Waging Peace

for a Living

CRISIS AS OPPORTUNITY
(wéi jī)

The Chinese word for *crisis* is made up of two parts:
danger and *opportunity*.

 Danger—originally pictured as a man on the edge of a precipice

 Opportunity—a reminder of the seemingly small but important opportunity that can come out of danger

This image has been taken from Calligraphy Presentations card line by Caravan International, Boulder, Colorado.

Waging Peace
for a Living

An action plan for
survival of life on earth

Walt Taylor

TRAFFORD

*Dedicated by Walt and Peggy Taylor
to our son Brian Taylor and our
grandson Gareth Chappe, two fine
men whose shortened lives were
full and wonderful.*

"Every day is a gift," Brian said.

Acknowledgments

For absolutely essential editorial assistance I want to thank a whole team of talented, sensitive, critical workers: Vigil Overstall put me in touch with all of them and helped us to get started; editor-in-chief Anne Maclean, Group of One Design, transformed my collection of ideas on paper into a respectable book; Will Lawson accomplished miracles with his talented ways of clarifying the organization of the text while enhancing its intent; Gerry Schreiber provided long-term encouragement and skillful assistance even when his studies and work kept him far away; Jeanie Elsner boosted the work with internet help and proofreading; Peggy Taylor, my wife, offered a wise, patient, penetrating, 20/20 review of my first drafts, never letting her legal blindness interfere with our collaboration. I take full responsibility for the results, however, whenever the author's final decisions prevailed over responsible, editorial suggestions.

For artistic work I am grateful, first, to Anne Maclean for the cover, for opening and concluding sketches, and for the sustained appearance throughout the book of the Chinese way of writing CRISIS, composed of one character for DANGER combined with another for OPPORTUNITY. Anne listens deeply and interprets artistically what she hears.

Art Wilson ('Wii Muk'willixw) is a Gitxsan artist and author of the beautiful and compassionate book *Heartbeat of the Earth: A First Nations Artist Records Injustice and Resistance*. I appreciate his friendship and his painting of our planet under stress. For the portrait of Albert Einstein I thank our friend, neighbour and art teacher, David Gillespie.

Many drawings, delightfully connected to the text, came from our long time friend on Cape Cod, Malcolm Wells. As an ecological architect, he has spent many years perfecting his special designs for preserving the environmental health and natural beauty of life above ground by creating safe, attractive, comfortable work and living spaces underground. I appreciate his dedication, sense of humour and generosity.

The cartoonists all speak for themselves, but I mention George Shane who gave me permission long ago to use his "Madam Minister . . .we find we can't afford survival!" I thank these skillful, relevant artists.

It is not possible to acknowledge all the friends and influences in my life that inspired me to write this book. I paid attention to scientific warnings throughout the past half century, and I have been thinking about responsive action plans for decades. Encouragement and stimulation came to me from many friends, including Jim Fulton, our former Member of Parliament and now Executive Director of The David Suzuki Foundation; William E. Rees, Director of the School of Community and Regional Planning at University of British Columbia; Ruben Bellan, author and economics professor emeritus in Winnipeg; scientist and ecological advocate David Suzuki.

In Chapter Notes I refer to many of the dedicated scientists, scholars and other writers whose wisdom I treasure. Now I acknowledge their remarkable contributions to survival and well-being for life on earth. I also thank everyone who reads this book and I acknowledge those who don't. Like the marvelous characters in the late Bill Reid's "Spirit of Haida Gwai," also known as "The Black Canoe"—we are all in the same boat.

危机 TABLE OF CONTENTS

危机 INTRODUCTION

Abandon Despair!

> Our nations across this Great Island, now called North
> America, continue to have an obligation to the Creator
> to care for and protect our lands for seven generations
> into the future. This obligation remains a sacred
> sacrament.
>
> —George Manuel, former President,
> Union of B.C. Indian Chiefs

The first law of ecology states that everything is connected to everything else. This book will touch on many things, but the connecting purpose for everything discussed here will be the survival and well-being of Mother Earth and the life which depends on her.

My motivation for writing this essay came from two stimulating sources—the extreme danger threatening our world in the twentieth century and the extraordinary opportunity beckoning to us as we enter the twenty-first.

Ever since World War II we have been receiving authoritative warnings from deeply concerned scientists and other profound thinkers. More than half a century ago, in 1946, Albert Einstein sent out a memorable but anguished message to the world:

> The unleashed power of the atom has changed
> everything save our modes of thinking, and thus we drift
> toward unparalleled catastrophe.[1]

The danger we now face is certainly daunting. At the same time a commensurate opportunity is opening up. An effective response to that extreme danger is not only necessary but also possible. By taking bold, responsible action to change our modes of thinking we have an exhilarating opportunity now to redirect our course away from unparalleled catastrophe toward survival, together with other priceless benefits. Now is the time for us to appreciate and take full advantage of this opportunity.

Waging Peace

Genuine peace demands far more than the mere absence of war, beneficial as that would certainly be for all life. Peace is the very antithesis of war, but waging peace and waging war do have much in common. Both call for high courage, training, apprenticeship, skill, imagination, cooperation, sacrifice, fortitude, dedication, and persistence—with invigorated ingenuity—in the face of disappointing setbacks.

Waging peace means planning and doing all the work required to inspire respect for our planet, recognition of the dangers we face, and acceptance of responsibility—like the responsibility assumed over scores of centuries by most aboriginal peoples—responsibility for the next seven generations of life on earth.

This book approaches the extraordinary dangers of our era as challenges to be translated into a catalogue of the specific work that must be done for the survival and well-being of our own and future generations.

In spite of many persuasive predictions that gloom and doom will overtake us in the twenty-first century, that will not happen unless we continue to belittle or ignore the warning signals so generously provided for us in the twentieth century.

Instead we can achieve joy and hope in abundance when we begin to make full use of our opportunities to keep this planet habitable and life worth living.

How can we do it?

In the following chapters I offer an action plan for survival of life on earth. Although I have great confidence in this proposal, I do not want readers to begin with any false or exaggerated expectations. This plan of mine is only a draft and it is wide open to improvement. Some individual or group may transform this proposal into a workable blueprint with many more details all figured out. Maybe some coalition of non-governmental organizations will even develop an entirely new plan, a better plan, and then take the first steps toward implementing it.

In the beginning I was deeply concerned about the wasteful extent of unemployment in Canada and around the world, especially tragic when there is so much necessary work right in front of us that is not yet being done. As this action plan developed further, however, the main purpose became clear: concentrate first on getting the urgently needed work underway. Then virtually full employment will follow naturally as an inevitable by-product of actually doing all this work that is absolutely essential for life.

This action plan emphasizes two complementary priorities: first, to identify the specific work that needs to be done and secondly, to invent ways to pay for it in spite of the deficit hysteria and the taxpayers' revolt which now prevent governments from financially supporting the work of preparing for enduring peace the way they have always provided whatever money was required to prepare for war.

We know there is lots of work to be done, although much of the most desperately needed work is non-profit. We know there is lots of money in the world, although an astonishing amount of it is held at present by a minority of wealthy people and corporations.

The action plan will begin with a year of research to identify the work that must be done and to invent realistic ways to provide enough financial support to pay for it.

For readers already familiar with the bad news

Some readers are already well aware of the many attempts by distinguished citizens of the world to document our unprecedented global predicament and to help us all understand that any effective response to these discomforting dangers will require bold—even revolutionary—changes in our modes of thinking, in our ways of living, and in our ways of earning a living. These readers may want to move directly to the action plan beginning in Chapter 2.

People who are *not* familiar with the increasingly dire warnings of our day may find them overwhelming at first, but I hope they will begin with Chapter 1 anyway. It provides the disturbing but absolutely necessary motivation for exploring what we can *do* about this danger. By facing facts squarely we can better appreciate that we have an enormous amount of work ahead of us and not much time left before our responsive action which is already too little might also become too late.

Good news

Virtually full employment across Canada and around the world will be a fortunate—even priceless—by-product of WAGING PEACE FOR A LIVING. Full employment is required for genuine peace as much as it has always been considered necessary for total, all-out war. Many of our worst problems, including financial deficits, will become far more tractable in a global climate of universal, meaningful, dignified employment.

This book is about the opportunities we now have available to us, unprecedented opportunities to discover, imagine, develop and invent unprecedented solutions to the unprecedented problems that confront humankind at this turn of the millennium.

I am simply transforming a horrible old warning attached to Dante's *Hell* into a warm invitation to readers of this book. Instead of "All hope abandon, ye who enter here,"[2] I suggest as soon as you turn this page:

ABANDON DESPAIR, ALL YE WHO ENTER HERE.

Notes

1. (a) Albert Einstein, quoted by Mike Moore, "Midnight Never Came" in *The Bulletin of the Atomic Scientists.* November/December 1995, pp. 16-27.
   On page 27 the quotation reads, "In May 1946, Albert Einstein, one of *The Bulletin*'s more notable godfathers, looked toward the future and said: 'The unleashed power of the atom has changed everything save our modes of thinking, and thus we drift toward unparalleled catastrophe.'"

   (b) Albert Einstein, a telegram to The New York Times on May 24, 1946, in the Oxford Dictionary of Quotations, New York: Oxford University Press, 1992, p. 268. This quotation reads, "The unleashed power of the atom has changed everything save our modes of thinking and we thus drift toward unparalled catastrophe."
   The development of atomic energy became possible through Einstein's own brilliant scientific work. During World War II he worried that the Nazis might take the lead in producing atomic bombs. He appealed to President Franklin Roosevelt for special effort to expedite atomic research in the United States. Later he expressed regret; had he known that German scientists would fail, he would not have lifted a finger to promote this intensive atomic bomb research. (See Chapter 1, Note 2.)

2. Dante Alighieri, translation by Henry Francis Cary, *Hell*, Canto III, line 9. Dante's life was from 1265 to 1321.

Facing page:

Asking For It

Over the centuries our people have lived by a particular philosophy and value system. This was to ensure that the balance of life be kept. All life forms have to be respected for they all have a purpose on earth.

In recent times, exploitation and greed have been the guiding principles of corporations. Politicians cater to them for it means jobs for their constituents.

In my opinion, we should not be so naive. The Earth is trying to tell us something. One has only to watch the news. Aren't we indeed "Asking For It" if we choose not to change our ways?

—'Wii Muk'willixw (Art Wilson)
The Bent Box, Kispiox, Gitxsan Territory

危机 CHAPTER 1

Dire Warnings of Unparalleled Catastrophe

> We are destroying the life support systems of this planet and threatening not only civilization as we know it but also the survival of our species.
> —Blue Planet Group, 1991

By now many people have already heard one version or another of the Great Frog Experiment. Wherever this story began, I first heard it from Maurice Strong when he was preparing to chair the 1972 United Nations Conference on the Human Environment in Stockholm, Sweden. Whether true or not, the reported behaviour of the frog in two desperate situations may help to explain our failure as human beings to respond appropriately as yet to extremely urgent warnings.

A team of researchers dropped an experimental frog right into a pan of boiling water. The frog obviously got the message because he instantly jumped out. Then these clever team members placed the frog in a pan of cool water. Under it they lit a Bunsen burner with the flame turned low. As the water warmed up slowly, the frog gradually became more and more comfortable. The water kept on getting hotter, however, and the frog relaxed so completely that he boiled to death.

This chapter is mainly for those readers who may have been too busy to notice the many increasingly disturbing reports over the past half century that our planet and its life are heading toward utter disaster in the twenty-first century unless we achieve some drastic changes soon in our ways of living, our ways of earning a living, and our willingness to share more equitably the only home we have, here on earth.

Paying close attention to these warnings now and responding to them with imagination and courageous action are necessary in order to justify any hope whatsoever for survival into the next millennium. The possibility of unparalleled catastrophe may seem inconceivable to many of us who enjoy relatively comfortable living in beautiful parts of the world. However, we may boil to death along with other people, plants, and animals if we continue to relax while our environmental and socio-economic crises warm up around us.

Some of us who do get the message may find the warnings just too painful, especially if they demand changes that seem way too far beyond human reach.

A half century of red, flashing alarms

The Worldwatch Institute declared in its annual report *State of the World 1989* that the 1990s must become a turnaround decade in human ways of living and ways of earning a living. The directors concluded that

> By the end of the next decade, the die will be pretty well cast. As the world enters the twenty-first century, the community of nations either will have rallied and turned back the threatening trends, or environmental deterioration and social disintegration will be feeding on each other.[1]

In the first half of the twentieth century, physicist Albert Einstein opened the way for scientists to understand and use the enormous power previously confined and unknown inside the atoms of matter. Distressed by Nazi atrocities and alarmed by the very real possibility that German scientists might become the first to develop atom bombs in their determination to rule the world, Dr. Einstein was persuaded to write an earnest letter to United States President

Franklin D. Roosevelt.[2] In response the President established the Manhattan Project for intensive research to produce atom bombs. The first two, the only nuclear weapons ever used in war to this day, virtually obliterated the Japanese cities of Hiroshima and Nagasaki on August 6 and 9, 1945.[3] This devastating slaughter of unarmed men, women, and children launched the first five decades of nuclear anguish around the world.

In a telegram to *The New York Times* on May 24, 1946, Einstein shared with the world his almost unthinkable foreboding:

> The unleashed power of the atom has changed everything save our modes of thinking, and thus we drift toward unparalleled catastrophe.[4]

Throughout the next half century the world received an impressive number of increasingly severe warnings from distinguished scientists and other forward thinkers. Some of these concerned world citizens were privileged and highly educated. Others, drawing on thousands of years of survival experience, provided us with a culturally different but equally powerful indigenous warning.

Silent Spring

In 1962 Rachel Carson published her *Silent Spring*. She began with Keats' "A sedge is wither'd from the lake, and no birds sing," and borrowed a summary word from E. B. White:

> I am pessimistic about the human race. . .because it is too ingenious for its own good. Our approach to nature is to beat it into submission. We would stand a better chance of survival if we accommodated ourselves to this planet and viewed it appreciatively instead of skeptically and dictatorially.

In conclusion, Carson wrote

> The 'control of nature' is a phrase conceived in
> arrogance, born of the Neanderthal age of biology and
> philosophy, when it was supposed that nature exists for
> the convenience of man. . . . It is our alarming misfortune
> that so primitive a science has armed itself with the most
> modern and terrible weapons, and that in turning them
> against the insects it has also turned them against the
> earth.[5]

A third of a century later, in 1996, a United Nations Environment
Programme report, *Taking Action*, identified some key facts about
biodiversity:

> An unprecedented mass extinction of life on Earth is
> occurring. Scientists estimate that between 150 and 200
> species of life become extinct every 24 hours. . . . this
> episode of species extinction is greater than anything
> the world has experienced for the past 65 million
> years—the greatest rate of extinction since the vanishing
> of the dinosaurs. Why? This mass extinction is due, in
> large measure, to humankind's unsustainable methods
> of production and consumption.[6]

Terracide

In 1970, environmentalist Ron M. Linton introduced a new word
as the title of his book, *Terracide: America's Destruction of Her Living
Environment*.[7] On the first page, just inside the cover, he provides a
chilling, dictionary-style definition:

> **ter′ra·cide′** (tĕr′a·sīd′), *n*.
> [L. *terra* the earth + *cae-*
> *dere* to kill.] 1. The ruin of
> the earth through man's
> actions and policies. 2.
> The act of destroying the
> earth. — *Ant.* Ecological
> harmony. — **terracidal,**
> *adj.*

In 1972 I spoke to the Housewives' College in Oliver, British Columbia, about troubled youth and delinquency, and also about our world committing terracide.[8] A quarter century later I am still unable to find the word "terracide" in any unabridged dictionary. Is such a frightful idea too unbelievable to justify dictionary recognition? Or is the concept just unspeakable?

In my speech I went beyond the assigned subject about troubled youth and delinquency. I explained that it is not only children and youth in our society who are troubled. The problem is our society is troubled. We keep finding ourselves trying to help children adjust to a crazy world. Maybe it is our society that needs adjusting.

Youth speaks

A twelve-year-old girl addressed a plenary session of the 1992 Earth Summit in Rio de Janeiro. On behalf of the Environmental Children's Organization, Severn Cullis-Suzuki said:

> We are a group of four 12 and 13 year olds from Canada trying to make a difference. . . .We raised all the money ourselves to come six thousand miles to tell you adults you must change your ways. . . . I'm only a child yet I know if all the money spent on war was spent on ending poverty and finding environmental answers, what a wonderful place this earth would be! . . . At school, even in kindergarten, you teach us to behave in the world. You teach us:
> - not to fight with others,
> - to work things out,
> - to respect others,
> - to clean up our mess,
> - not to hurt other creatures,
> - to share—not be greedy.
>
> Then why do you go out and do the things you tell us not to do? . . .You grown ups say you love us. I challenge you, please, make your actions reflect your words.[9]

In my speech twenty years earlier, I announced that experts would meet in Stockholm for the United Nations Conference on the

Human Environment in June 1972 to study the profound changes required in human values and priorities in order to stop destroying nature on which life depends.[10]

The partners in this adult delinquency, I said, are the powerful, affluent, highly educated, scientifically and technologically advanced people on earth, namely us. To the extent that the under-developed billions of people on earth struggle to be like us—the over-developed 1 billion people—they will be learning the arts and crafts of terracide. To the extent that we the over-developed people refuse to de-develop, we persist in attempted terracide, and we are getting close to successfully executing this ultimate human crime.

I acknowledged that many people at that time might be skeptical about all these warnings that the world was facing some utter "disaster." However, I suggested, "If the alarms prove false or excessive, the only consequence that could result from heeding them would be an improvement in the quality of life for generations to come."

Three messages from science

On May 11, 1971, a quarter century after Einstein's warning, and just prior to the Stockholm Conference, Secretary-General of the United Nations U Thant received *A Message to Our 3.5 Billion Neighbours on Planet Earth from 2,200 Environmental Scientists.* By 1973 some 4,000 scientists from 40 countries had signed this message. It is not only still relevant now in a world of nearly 6 billion neighbours, but it has also become far more urgent in the 1990s.

The problems detailed in the message included environmental deterioration, depletion of natural resources, population, overcrowding and hunger, and war.

> Widely separated though we are geographically, with very different cultures, languages, attitudes, political and religious loyalties, we are united in our time by an unprecedented common danger. This danger, of a nature and magnitude never before faced by man, is born of a confluence of several phenomena. Each of them would

present us with almost unmanageable problems: together they present not only the probability of vast increases in human suffering in the immediate future, but the possibility of the extinction, or virtual extinction, of human life on Earth. As biological and other environmental scientists, we do not speak to the feasibility of particular solutions to these problems, but out of our conviction that the problems exist, are global and interrelated, and that solutions can be found only if we abandon limited selfish interests to the realization of a common need.[11]

In September 1991, the Blue Planet Group of sixty distinguished Canadians published their one-page appeal for a *Blue Planet: Now or Never!* They reported that we are destroying the life-support systems of this planet and endangering the very survival of our species. One billion relatively comfortable people in the North use 10 times more resources and produce 10 times more waste per capita, compared to 4 billion poor people in the South. "We live on a finite planet and are part of nature," they wrote. "Human activities are the most dynamic and threatening force in the biosphere." Nevertheless, their statement encourages us to "recognize that we cannot go on as before, and embark immediately and deliberately upon a bold course of global ecological sustainability." The Blue Planet Group called for "an unparalleled revolution in our way of thinking about our future."[12]

The David Suzuki Foundation has declared,

There's a lot to do. . . .We're faced with the necessity for rapid, fundamental change. The beliefs and attitudes that underlie our society have brought us to the brink of disaster. We are learning some hard lessons: the earth's resources are not limitless, the economy cannot continue to grow forever, and we are part of Nature, not superior to it.[13]

World Scientists' Warning to Humanity

In 1992 nearly 1,700 of the world's leading scientists, from 71 different countries, including 104 Nobel laureates, signed a two-page *World Scientists' Warning to Humanity*.

We the undersigned, senior members of the world's scientific community, hereby warn all humanity of what lies ahead. A great change in our stewardship of the earth and the life on it is required if vast human misery is to be avoided and our global home on this planet is not to be irretrievably mutilated.

. . . Human beings and the natural world are on a collision course. Human activities inflict harsh and often irreversible damage on the environment and on critical resources. If not checked, many of our current practices put at risk the future that we wish for human society and the plant and animal kingdoms, and may so alter the living world that it will be unable to sustain life in the manner that we know. . . .

The Atmosphere Stratospheric ozone depletion threatens us with enhanced ultraviolet radiation at the earth's surface, which can be damaging or lethal to many life forms. Air pollution near ground level, and acid precipitation, are already causing widespread injury to humans, forests, and crops.

Water Resources Heedless exploitation of depletable ground water supplies endangers food production and other essential human systems. Heavy demands on the world's surface waters have resulted in serious shortages in some 80 countries, containing 40 percent of the world's population. Pollution of rivers, lakes and ground water further limits the supply.

Oceans Destructive pressure on the oceans is severe, particularly in the coastal regions which produce most of the world's food fish. The total marine catch is now at or above the estimated maximum sustainable yield. Some fisheries have already shown signs of collapse. Rivers carrying heavy burdens of eroded soil into the seas also carry industrial, municipal, agricultural, and livestock waste—some of it toxic.

Soil Loss of soil productivity, which is causing extensive land abandonment, is a widespread by-product of current practices in agriculture and animal husbandry. Since 1945, 11 percent of the earth's vegetated surface has been degraded—an area larger than India and China combined—and per capita food production in many parts of the world is decreasing.

Forests Tropical rain forests, as well as tropical and temperate dry forests, are being destroyed rapidly. At present rates, some critical forest types will be gone in a few years, and most of the tropical rain forest will be gone before the end of the next century. With them will go large numbers of plant and animal species.

Living Species The irreversible loss of species, which by 2100 may reach one-third of all species now living, is especially serious. We are losing the potential they hold for providing medicinal and other benefits, and the contribution that genetic diversity of life forms gives to the robustness of the world's biological systems and to the astonishing beauty of the earth itself.

Much of this damage is irreversible on a scale of centuries, or permanent. Other processes appear to pose additional threats. Increasing levels of gases in the atmosphere from human activities, including carbon dioxide released from fossil fuel burning and from deforestation, may alter climate on a global scale. Predictions of global warming are still uncertain—with projected effects ranging from tolerable to very severe—but the potential risks are very great.

Our massive tampering with the world's interdependent web of life—coupled with the environmental damage inflicted by deforestation, species loss, and climate change—could trigger widespread adverse effects, including unpredictable collapse of critical biological systems whose interactions and dynamics we only imperfectly understand.

Uncertainty over the extent of these effects cannot excuse complacency or delay in facing the threats.

Population The earth is finite. Its ability to absorb wastes and destructive effluent is finite. Its ability to provide food and energy is finite. Its ability to provide for growing numbers of people is finite. And we are fast approaching many of the earth's limits. Current economic practices which damage the environment, in both developed and under-developed nations, cannot be continued without the risk that vital global systems will be damaged beyond repair.

Pressures resulting from unrestrained population growth put demands on the natural world that can overwhelm any efforts to achieve a sustainable future. If we are to halt the destruction of our environment, we must accept limits to that growth. A World Bank estimate indicates that world population will not stabilize at less than 12.4 billion, while the United Nations concludes that the eventual total could reach 14 billion, a near tripling of today's 5.4 billion. But, even at this moment, one person in five lives in absolute poverty, without enough to eat, and one in ten suffers serious malnutrition.

NO MORE THAN ONE OR A FEW DECADES REMAIN before the chance to avert the threats we now confront will be lost and the prospects for humanity immeasurably diminished.[14] [My emphasis]

Fourth anniversary of World Scientists' Warning

In recognition of the fourth anniversary of this extraordinary warning to humanity, CBC Radio (Canadian Broadcasting Corporation) did a special programme about it in November 1996.[15]

Henry Kendall is chair of the Union of Concerned Scientists which initiated the warning, and a Nobel Prize winning physics professor at Massachusetts Institute of Technology. He thinks we are playing with fire when we tamper with the earth's life support systems and believes that matters are getting more and more grave.

David Suzuki was even more blunt. He is a biologist specializing in the field of genetics, and host of CBC's remarkable weekly programme on TV, *The Nature of Things*. On the fourth anniversary radio programme he said,

> I think the disaster is already here. A few years ago when Jean Charest was Canada's Minister of the Environment, he told us that on a sunny day we should keep our children in. My wife railed at that! She said, 'For God's sake, in Canada a sunny day is a day to go out and celebrate and now our Minister of Environment is saying that's a day to be afraid because of the ultraviolet rays and thinning of the ozone layer.' We've hit the wall, for Heaven's sake!

David Suzuki also criticized the media for not paying more attention to a warning by so many prominent scientists:

> CBC never carried it; the Toronto Globe and Mail didn't cover it; in the United States the Washington Post and the New York Times both rejected it as not newsworthy. So, when half of all the Nobel Prize winners say that civilization may end in ten years and this is ignored, that's an absolute scandal!

Geologist Digby McLaren is a past president of the Royal Society of Canada, and a former science advisor to UNESCO. He was part of the group that wrote *Blue Planet: Now or Never!* He signed the *World Scientists' Warning to Humanity* and spoke out in the fourth anniversary programme:

> We're facing a catastrophe now. We are actually in a catastrophe. When I was born, seventy-six years ago, the population of the earth was just a little bit less than 1.8 billion. And if I live to be eighty, then it will be 6 billion. Now that's unique. There's never been anything like that. So that we are in the middle of a growing curve. And the use of energy is going up exponentially now. So we are in the crisis. And, of course, there are secondary problems coming out of that: instabilities, increase of refugees and so on; perhaps the nastiest of all is the growth in disparity between rich and poor.

Digby McLaren is decidedly pessimistic about the future facing mankind. "This worries me dreadfully," he said, "that I personally have very little hope. . . . Of course, I laughingly say that I'm glad I'm as old as I am, but I'm not really. I've got children and grandchildren and they're all quite aware of this, and I suffer with them."

At the conclusion of the CBC broadcast we heard:

> Scientist James Lovelock has proposed a theory that the planet earth may itself be one complex, living organism involving the biosphere, atmosphere, oceans, and soil. He named it Gaia after the Greek goddess of the Earth. But Gaia, or Mother Nature if you will, can be very stern and cruel. Perhaps the 'Scientists' Warning to Humanity' is telling us that she can only be pushed so far.

Our ecological footprint

The year 1996 began with a book titled *Our Ecological Footprint: Reducing Human Impact on the Earth* by Mathis Wackernagel and William Rees.[16] It offered an impressive way to get the feel of our increasingly heavy, human footsteps on Earth. The concept of an "ecological footprint" was based on years of scholarly study and concern by co-author Rees, Director of the School of Community and Regional Planning at the University of British Columbia.

The authors have developed a way to measure the human threat to survival and well-being, and some very urgent reasons for people to tread more lightly on the Earth. One's "footprint" is the area of the planet required to provide what one consumes and to assimilate one's contribution to global waste. It is useful to consider an *average* footprint—globally, regionally, or in any one particular community— while keeping in mind that *individual* footprints vary enormously in size and impact.

In today's world, the top 20 percent of income earners take home over sixty times more than the poorest 20 percent. In order to provide everyone on Earth with the same standard of living as the average North American, the authors estimate that "we would need at least three such planets to live sustainably."[17]

Since the beginning of the twentieth century, however,

> the available ecologically productive land has decreased from over five hectares to less than 1.5 hectares per person in 1994. At the same time, the average North American's Footprint has grown to over four hectares. These opposing trends are in fundamental conflict: the ecological demands of average citizens in rich countries exceed per capita supply by a factor of three.[18]

At the latest available report, the number of billionaires in the world increased from 145 in 1987 to 358 in 1994. A small minority, only 6 trillionths of the world's people, have accumulated for themselves US$ 761.9 billion. They have as much wealth as the total annual per capita income of 45 percent of the people on Earth, about 2.6 billion people.[19]

On the other hand, some 10 million people die of starvation every year in our modern world.

Turning the tide

I have excerpted the following quotations from John Dillon's 1997 book, *Turning the Tide: Confronting the Money Traders*.[20] In writing the book John Dillon represents the Toronto-based Ecumenical Coalition for Economic Justice. "The purpose of this book is to show that we have other options. . . ," he wrote. "We shall show that we need not be ruled by the power of global financiers."

> Over the past two decades, the world economy has entered a radically new phase. . . . In this new stage of capitalism there is no longer a commitment to full employment and enhanced social welfare. . . .The Bank for International Settlements estimates that the pool of 'hot money' that can flow instantaneously around the world through telecommunications networks amounts to US$ 13 trillion. . . . daily transactions total some US$ 4 trillion. Most of these transactions are speculative. . . .

Speculators grow very wealthy doing nothing more tangible than rearranging zeroes and ones on computer chips as they buy and sell cybermoney. Meanwhile, much of what is truly valuable, that which sustains human life and natural ecosystems, is treated as valueless unless it can be bought and sold as a commodity. . . .

The misery of the unemployed and the wealth accumulated by financial investors are directly related. The Bank of Canada, our central bank, deliberately pursues policies that keep unemployment high as a means of curtailing inflation. The principal beneficiaries of these policies are financial investors who profit from high real (that is, inflation-adjusted) interest rates. . . . When the wealth gap within countries is taken into account, the richest 20% of the world's people are 150 times more affluent than the poorest 20%. . . .

Some 30 percent of the world's labour force, representing 820 million people, are counted as unemployed by the International Labour Organization.

Most official data on employment and income distribution ignore the contribution made by women's unpaid work in the home and in subsistence agriculture. For the high rollers of world finance, people are becoming less important—both as producers and as consumers. Latin Americans no longer speak about the millions who live in absolute poverty as the 'marginalized,' since this term implies that sooner or later they might be incorporated into the mainstream of society. Instead they now speak about 'the excluded' masses who neither produce for the world economy nor consume from it. In Columbia the excluded have even been described as 'the disposable ones'. . . . These financiers demand that governments fight the spectre of inflation through high interest rates and high unemployment, and cut spending to reduce their deficits. . . . we believe that, if we try to play by the rules set by the financiers, we risk everything we hold sacred: our social programs, the integrity of our environment, and even our compassion and our humanity.[21]

The Doomsday Clock

In 1995 the Norwegian Nobel Committee awarded its annual Peace Prize in equal parts to Joseph Rotblat and the Pugwash Conferences on Science and World Affairs. It wanted to "encourage world leaders to intensify their efforts to rid the world of nuclear weapons."[22]

The *World Scientists' Warning to Humanity* did not include the unleashed power of the atom among its listed perils for humankind. Just after World War II, the *Bulletin of the Atomic Scientists* began as a series of newsletters with no magazine-style covers. The June 1947 issue, however, bore an arresting orange cover on which readers found the first "Doomsday Clock" with the hour hand at 12:00 and the minute hand at about seven minutes to. An editorial in the July 1947 issue said the clock "represents the state of mind of those whose closeness to the development of atomic energy does not permit them to forget that their lives and those of their children, the security of their country and the survival of civilization, all hang in the balance as long as the specter of atomic war has not been exorcized. . . . Humankind," the clock said, "was in dire straits."

Every bi-monthly issue still carries the clock. For the past five decades that clock has been warning the world that nuclear arms might lead to nuclear war and thus to the end of civilization.

The hands on this symbol of the nuclear peril facing humankind have been moved forward and back 15 times, ranging between two minutes to midnight and seventeen minutes to midnight, according to changes in the Cold War and other critical international circumstances.[23]

On December 8, 1995, the board of the *Bulletin of the Atomic Scientists* moved the hands forward to fourteen minutes to midnight, even though the Cold War was over. The Board Statement acknowledged that there had been "grounds for optimism" in 1991, but

> in the past four years, it has become clear that opportunities have been missed, open doors closed. . . . The United States and Russia collectively possess more than 35,000 nuclear weapons. . . . No new arms reduction

treaties are in the works. . . . The chemical and biological weapons conventions have not been ratified by the United States and Russia. Beyond issues of weapons of mass destruction, the world remains an exceptionally brutish place. Genocide is on the evening news. The United Nations, humankind's best hope for stopping such violence, has failed to fulfill our expectations, in part because the major powers have not gotten fully behind peacekeeping efforts. The growing gap between rich and poor is fueling desperation and conflict.

The worldwide arms trade continues to boom, and many of the world's nations—including the United States—continue to divert huge amounts of intellectual and monetary capital into military enterprises and useless military hardware.

Yes, the world extended the Nuclear Non-Proliferation Treaty last May [1995]. And next year, the world may get a comprehensive test ban treaty. But on balance, the world is still a very dangerous place, and trends are all in the wrong direction. . . . We do want to call for increased vigilance. Today, we move the minute hand of the clock back onto the scale—to 14 minutes to midnight.[24]

In a letter to me on January 28, 1997, the editor of the *Bulletin*, Mike Moore, wrote that he saw no contradiction between the *World Scientists' Warning to Humanity* by the Union of Concerned Scientists and the work of the *Bulletin*.

In its statement, UCS is trying to focus attention on some very grave environmental threats to humankind. Meanwhile, the Bulletin reminds people that nuclear weapons—which are not essentially environmental threats—still pose a very great risk. After all, some 40,000 weapons still remain in the world's arsenals, and the major nuclear powers retain many thousands of weapons on alert. . . .The problem of nuclear weapons is not so much environmental—but in their possible use. If used in great numbers, much of modern civilization would be destroyed. . . . we try to serve the world by reminding people that nuclear weapons may have been swept under the rug, so to speak, but they are still around in awesomely dangerous numbers.

For many years "peaceful" nuclear energy was promoted as "safe, clean, and too cheap to metre." In a 1997 article, David Orchard earnestly opposed any Canadian plans to accept U.S. nuclear waste and to "test burn" a shipment of U.S. plutonium on a Candu reactor:

> The U.S. Department of Energy acknowledged the Candu is untested at 'burning' plutonium but added: "There may be less public resistance than in the United States." That half the plutonium would still exist after being 'burned,' and that the waste would become Canada's responsibility, was downplayed.
>
> High level nuclear waste, the by-product of nuclear power reactors and nuclear weapons, contains some of the most deadly poisons known. Some will remain so for a million years. For example, plutonium, an entirely man-made substance, is created only in nuclear reactors, and a minute speck in the lung (invisible to the eye) is enough to cause cancer. . . .
>
> Burying nuclear waste is a declaration of the failure of science. Dumping deadly toxins in the ocean, into the atmosphere or underground simply leaves unsuspecting future generations to cope with the inevitable catastrophic leakage.
>
> Burial is a political strategy. If the nuclear industry can present the public with a 'solution' (out of sight, out of mind) to its most serious problem, then it can continue, and even expand, its production of lethal waste. Burial means precious little research will be done by the industry on neutralization, and nuclear powers will line up to dump their waste.[25]

Climate change

In an urgent 1997 communication, The David Suzuki Foundation described climate change as "the key issue of this century, yet 'they' say: it's too costly to do anything; it's too hard for Canadians to change; it's too difficult for people to understand." David Suzuki believes 'they' are wrong.

> World scientists now agree that human beings are changing the climate. Burning carbon fuels like oil and

coal creates greenhouse gases, which are heating the planet too rapidly for the natural environment and human societies to adapt. . . .

To slow and ultimately reverse the impacts of Global Warming, emissions must be reduced from current levels—and must keep falling. . . .

The world's most distinguished scientists working on climate change conclude that 10-30% reductions in energy consumption are possible at no cost to the economy, just through greater energy efficiency. . . .

Increasing global temperature leads to catastrophic changes in climate. Scientists expect rising sea levels and flooding, human disease outbreaks, droughts, crop failures, forest fires, and extreme storms.[26]

Are poor people worth less?

Some prestigious economists developed an outrageous cost-benefit analysis to show that it will cost less for the world simply to accept the impact of climate change than to take the action which scientists consider necessary to prevent global warming, by cutting back the emission of greenhouse gases. These economists are in Working Group 3 (WG3) of the Intergovernmental Panel on Climate Change.

Their so-called "Willingness to Pay" method of assessing damage asked, "How much are people willing to pay for a better environment?" People in the South, those not in the wealthier OECD countries (Organization for Economic Cooperation and Development), were classified as "Rest of the World". These people make up 80 percent of the world's population and live on 80 percent of the world's surface area.

For their controversial cost-benefit analysis these WG3 economists put dollar values on human life. People in the industrialized, rich North, they say, are worth $1.5 million each, while poorer people in the South are worth only $150,000 each.

The people in the South are much more vulnerable to the ravages of global warming, but they are also worth less. When you add it all up, the cost-benefit analysis favours accepting the damage from climate change because most of the people who will be harmed or killed are expendable, each one being "worth" so much less in dollar value while Europeans and North Americans are "worth"10 times as much.[27]

This "expert" judgment that poor people are dispensable because they are worth less than other people has been vigorously challenged by competent critics, but the very existence of such an attitude among some influential economists is alarming. They show contempt not only for poor people, but also for the health of our planet. They impose on concerned people one more obstacle to undertaking all the work required to reduce global greenhouse gas emissions sufficiently to prevent disastrous worsening of the danger of global warming.

Warnings based on hundreds of centuries of aboriginal experience

Some of the warnings that have come to us in the twentieth century have ancient roots in aboriginal experience and belief systems which combine social, economic, ecological, scientific, philosophical, recreational, and spiritual aspects of life into a holistic worldview.

Handicapped by cultural deafness, blindness, insensitivity, and arrogance over the past 500 years, too many non-aboriginal people have been unable to appreciate this valuable heritage of ancient but still relevant indigenous wisdom.

From the Heart of the World is a film produced by Alan Ereira for the British Broadcasting Corporation. The Kogi tribe granted one-time-only permission for a film crew to visit in order to allow us, "The Younger Brothers," to receive "The Elder Brothers' Warning". The nature of this Kogi message is suggested in the text on the film's cover:

> This is the last civilization of pre-Columbian America that vanished 400 years ago. It did not die—it went into hiding. For centuries the Kogi have watched us from their mountain fastness. This film is their message, and their warning. . . .

Deep in the [Andes] mountains of Columbia, the descendants of an ancient Tairona priesthood still rule. In cities more than a thousand years old, the ascetic Kogi tribe has preserved the culture and spirituality of an advanced civilization wiped out by the conquistadors.

Situated close to the equator, only 26 miles from the beach, their mountain region contains nearly every ecosystem found on earth. Evidence of environmental damage can be readily seen from their mountainous vantage point. Global warming has melted snow, and what was once high tundra is now dust. After centuries of deliberate isolation, the Kogi have decided that the time has come to speak to us about these changes.

Through concentrated thought and meditation, the Kogi enter an inner-plane world called aluna and act there. Aluna was and is the Mother, whose law is harmony and balance. The whole of Kogi life revolves around this life force that shapes the world and makes it flower.

They call themselves the Elder Brothers of the human race, and are convinced that we, the Younger Brothers, will soon destroy the balance of life on Earth. They believe that the only hope is for us to change our ways, and have set out to teach us what they know about the balance of mankind, nature and the spiritual world.[28]

From the Iroquois Confederacy, the Hau de no sau nee, the traditional Six Nations council at Onondaga, New York, responded to a request by Non-Governmental Organizations of the United Nations for a series of position papers which they presented in Geneva in September 1977. *A Basic Call to Consciousness: The Hau de no sau nee Address to the Western World* was published the following year.

The Hau de no sau nee warning has ancient roots. The delegation reported in part:

The Western culture has been horribly exploitative and destructive of the Natural World. Over 140 species of birds and animals were utterly destroyed since the European arrival in the Americas, largely because they were unusable in the eyes of the invaders. The forests were levelled, the waters polluted, the Native people subjected to genocide. The vast herds of herbivores were reduced to mere handfuls, the buffalo nearly became extinct. Western technology and the people who have employed it have been the most amazingly destructive forces in all of human history. No natural disaster has ever destroyed as much. Not even the Ice Ages counted as many victims.

But like the hardwood forests, the fossil fuels are also finite resources. As the second half of the Twentieth Century has progressed, the people of the West have begun looking to other forms of energy to motivate their technology. Their eyes have settled on atomic energy, a form of energy production which has by-products which are the most poisonous substances ever known to Man.

Today the species of Man is facing a question of the very survival of the species. The way of life known as Western Civilization is on a death path to which their own culture has no viable answers. When faced with the reality of their own destructiveness, they can only go forward into areas of more efficient destruction. The appearance of Plutonium on this planet is the clearest of signals that our species is in trouble. It is a signal which most Westerners have chosen to ignore.

The air is foul, the waters polluted, the trees dying, the animals are disappearing. We think even the systems of weather are changing. Our ancient teachings warned us that if Man interfered with Natural laws, these things would come to be. When the last of the Natural Way of Life is gone, all hope for human survival will be gone with it. And our Way of Life is fast disappearing, a victim of the destructive processes. . . .[29]

The Iroquois worldview shares a common concern with all aboriginal people around the world. Many appeals for public understanding and help resemble the following statement on behalf of the Hopi and Navajo traditional peoples in the southwestern United States:

Their land, water, culture, and rights are all threatened to be destroyed forever in America's quest for energy sources. Half of America's uranium and one-third of its western coal reserves are on Indian land. . . .The government and multi-national energy companies are beginning the final genocidal assault on the remaining land base of America's Native people. The energy companies' profits will come from the final rip-off of Indian land, water, and resources, which were guaranteed to the Indian Nations forever by the treaties.

The indigenous peoples of the world have an inherent right to survival. The relocation of the Navajo denies that right. The real cost of removal is the destruction of the people. Indian land claims to land occupied by whites have all been settled with money compensation. To evict a white man would be unthinkable. This time, however, Indians occupy the 'claimed' land and somehow, eviction, removal, and relocation becomes acceptable. . . .

There is an alternative to relocation, and that is repeal of the law which is creating this injustice and tragedy for the native peoples of northern Arizona. All people should be alarmed that any Indian people for any reason could be forceably removed from their lands. Those same economic, social, and political forces which are destroying their lives surely will destroy others.

In the words of Thomas Banyacya, interpreter for the traditional Hopi religious leaders, "What is happening at Big Mountain today is a warning. If these sacred lands are disrupted and the Navajos driven off the land this will signal the 'longest walk to death' for the Navajo and Hopi peoples. If this sacred land is abused and ripped apart by mineral exploitation and other destructive activities this in the long run will also signal the 'longest walk to death' for all peoples of the world."[30]

Even after many generations of cultural battering—social, educational, economic, environmental, spiritual, and even physical and sexual abuse or outright destruction—the ancient wisdom has survived. A growing appreciation of this aboriginal heritage will help in opening the way for survival and well-being of the earth and its life in the twenty-first century and beyond. Indigenous people are certainly among the most experienced survivors the world has ever known.[31]

Red, flashing warning signals keep telling us to stop, look, and listen while we begin to transform our awareness of extreme danger into appropriate responsive action. Thousands of years of aboriginal wisdom combined with half a century of increasingly severe Western scientific warnings make it possible for us now to confront our predicament openly and to stop drifting—or being jet-propelled—"toward unparalleled catastrophe." Gloom and doom need not overpower us unless we ignore the warnings.

Dangers and opportunities

The unprecedented challenges we face as we approach a new millennium include many other urgent problems in addition to the almost overwhelming environmental dangers. Rocket science has given space a new meaning. Human beings have landed on the moon with dreams of colonizing Mars. Medical miracles continue to amaze us. Now, before many of us have had time to catch our breath, we are already speeding along the information highways of cyberspace.

What happens now to our old military and police concepts of "security" in this new world of land mines, nuclear and biological weaponry, systematic torture, massacre, starvation, and genocide which is now euphemized as "ethnic cleansing?"

The "free trade" gospel that is being promoted for the whole world by a small but powerful minority would widen still further the already enormous chasm between rich and poor while totally ignoring human rights and all the warnings that a major change is desperately needed in our ways of living and earning a living if we are to avoid unparalleled social and environmental catastrophe.

We must make fundamental changes in our approach to economics, energy, health, science and technology, human rights, housing, agriculture, forestry, fishing, mining, banking, political systems, spiritual development, conflict resolution, media, manufacturing, international cooperation, and above all else, cultivating respect for the earth.

The planet and its life cannot tolerate the continued corporate domination of the media, employment, energy, tax systems, transportation and global policies that enhance and protect the very affluent at enormous expense to other people, the earth, and future generations.

Among our most significant discoveries of the past century, two are gradually kindling hope for the future. One is a growing understanding among us about the dark side of progress. We find that some of our most extreme dangers have emerged from advances in Western science and technology during the twentieth century. At the same time we are beginning to appreciate the modern relevance of aboriginal knowledge, experience, humour, and spirit for living in harmony with nature and with respect for the planet.

We can benefit from this increasing awareness of some savage aspects in our advanced industrial civilization and some civilizing opportunities in ancient but still vital cultures that were previously scorned as "savage."

In order to explore the opportunities before us to allow everyone on earth to gain much more than anyone loses, turn now to the rest of the book for a proposed action plan.

Notes

1. Lester R. Brown, Christopher Flavin and Sandra Postel, "A Turnaround Decade" in Chapter 10, "Outlining a Global Action Plan," in Worldwatch Institute, *State of the World 1989*, New York: W. W. Norton, 1989, p. 194.

2. Karl Grossman, *Cover Up: What you are not supposed to know about Nuclear Power*, Sagaponack, New York: The Permanent Press, 1980.
    The first letter from Albert Einstein to President Franklin D. Roosevelt in 1939 is explained on page 24. The second letter, dated August 2, 1939, is discussed and a copy presented on pages 151-153. "Einstein would later regret what he did." In retrospect he wrote, "If I had known that the Germans would not succeed in constructing the atom bomb, I never would have moved a finger."

3. The Committee for the Compilation of Materials on Damage Caused by the Atomic Bombs in Hiroshima and Nagasaki, *Hiroshima and Nagasaki: The Physical, Medical, and Social Effects of the Atomic Bombings*, originally published in Japanese by Iwanami Shoten, Tokyo, 1979; copyright 1981 by Hiroshima City and Nagasaki City.
    This book is "the definitive scientific report on Hiroshima and Nagasaki— the only experience we've had to date with nuclear warfare." The Appendix includes "The City of Hiroshima Peace Declaration, August 6, 1980" by Takeshi Araki, Mayor of Hiroshima, and "The City of Nagasaki Peace Declaration, August 9, 1980" by Hitoshi Motoshima, Mayor of Nagasaki.

4. *Op. cit.*, Introduction, Note 1.

5. Rachel Carson, *Silent Spring*, New York: Houghton Mifflin, 1962, pp. 261-262.

6. *Taking Action: An Environmental Guide for You and Your Community*, Nairobi, Kenya: Published by the United Nations Environment Programme in association with the United Nations Non-Governmental Liaison Service, 1996. Chapter 10, "Biodiversity, Key Facts," p. 129.

7. Ron M. Linton, *Terracide: America's Destruction of Her Living Environment*, New York: Paperback Library Edition published by arrangement with Little, Brown and Company, copyright 1970, Paperback Library, 1971.

8. Sonni Bone, Women's Editor, "World Facing Disaster, Attempting 'Terracide,'" in *The Penticton Herald*, Penticton, British Columbia, February 25, 1972.

9. Severn Cullis-Suzuki, *Tell the World: A Young Environmentalist Speaks Out,*
    Toronto: Doubleday, 1993, pp. 9, 23, 24 and 26.

10. (a) The Stockholm Conference on the Human Environment,
       Stockholm, Sweden, June 5 to 12, 1972, chaired by Maurice Strong.

    (b) Walter Taylor, "A Concern for Consideration by the Canadian Delegates
        to the United Nations Conference on the Human Environment,"
        April 24, 1972.
        ". . .Alternatives can be discovered and invented to keep our planet
        habitable and to permit a continually improving quality of life.
        ". . .Over-developed people must find satisfying ways to live without
        consuming more than their share of resources and without producing
        intolerable environmental destruction.
        "In North America the Indian heritage contains much of the wisdom,
        the humor, the reverence for the earth and the spirit of living in harmony
        with the rest of nature which will be necessary for future survival. In
        spite of all the cultural damage they have suffered, many North American
        Indians could serve the United Nations well as experts on survival and
        specialists in sustaining a high quality of life without destroying the human
        environment.
        "Other less developed people on earth also retain these gifts for living
        in equilibrium without cancerous economic and population growth.
        "I hope the Canadian delegates will urge the Stockholm Conference
        to seek guidance for the future among such gifted people with thousands
        of years of inherited experience in how to live richly satisfying lives
        without fouling their own nest."

11. "A Message to Our 3.5 Billion Neighbors on Planet Earth from 2,200
    Environmental Scientists" was published in *The UNESCO Courier*
    (United Nations Educational, Scientific and Cultural Organization) in July,
    1971.
    This "Menton Statement" was originally drafted in Menton, France, in
    1970 at a meeting of scientists convened by the International Fellowship of
    Reconciliation and a non-governmental, transnational peace movement
    known as *Dai Dong*. Literally, the name *Dai Dong* means "a world of the
    great togetherness," a concept which originated in pre-Confucian China more
    than 2,500 years prior to this "Message . . ."
    Six distinguished scientists presented the message to UN Secretary-General
    U Thant on May 11, 1971. In his response, he said, ". . .This global concern
    in the face of a grave common danger, which carries the seeds of extinction
    for the human species, may well prove to be the elusive force which can

bind men together. The battle for human survival can only be won by all nations joining together in a concerted drive to preserve life on this planet."

By 1973 some 4,000 scientists from 40 different countries had signed this statement. By 1997 "our 3.5 billion neighbors on Planet Earth" had grown to 5.8 billion! The "Message" still remains essentially valid today, but it has become more urgent in the 1990s.

12. Blue Planet Group, *"Blue Planet: Now or Never—A Statement,"* Ottawa: September 1991.

"This paper was prepared by a group of concerned [Canadian] citizens who gave their opinion without affiliation to any institution or agency, and with no particular philosophy or sociological position. They cover a wide range of disciplines and knowledge, and are convinced of the need to take some action at this moment in human development." The Blue Planet Group, Box 9734, Ottawa, Ontario K1G 5J4.

13. The David Suzuki Foundation brochure, 1992.

14. (a) *World Scientists' Warning to Humanity*, sponsored by the Union of Concerned Scientists, Two Brattle Square, Cambridge, Massachusetts 02238-9105, December 1992.

(b) Co-sponsored by the Union of Concerned Scientists and the World Bank, "Meeting the Challenges of Population, Environment, and Resources—The Costs of Inaction: A Report of the Senior Scientists' Panels," An Associated Event of the Third Annual World Bank Conference on Environmentally Sustainable Development, Environmentally Sustainable Development Proceedings Series No. 14, Washington, D. C.: The World Bank, September 1996. (Appendix A is the full text of "World Scientists' Warning to Humanity, pp. 41-45.)

(c) Karen Mortimer, Canadian Global Change Program, "Scientists' Warning to Humanity" in *Delta: Newsletter of the Canadian Global Change Program*, Vol. 4, No. 2, Summer 1993.

"About 1700 senior scientists from 71 different countries—including 104 Nobel laureates—are so concerned about the threat of environmental degradation that they have gone public and signed the now well known World Scientists' Warning to Humanity."

Beyond the warning, "The statement goes on to make five suggestions as to 'what we must do,' from bringing environmentally damaging activities under control, to managing resources more effectively, to reducing and eventually eliminating poverty. . . ."

15. On the fourth anniversary of "World Scientists' Warning to Humanity" a CBC Radio programme (Canadian Broadcasting Corporation) devoted its "Focus" programme on November 23,1996, to a recognition of that warning. The programme brought the warning to public attention after it had been virtually ignored or even rejected by much of the mainstream media ever since it was first announced. The broadcast was transcribed by Walt Taylor.

16. Mathis Wackernagel and William E. Rees, Illustrated by Phil Testemale, *Our Ecological Footprint: Reducing Human Impact on the Earth*, Gabriola Island, British Columbia: New Society Publishers, 1996.

17. *Ibid.*, p. 13.

18. *Ibid.*, p. 14.

19. *Forbes*, July 1994, cited in "World Bank and IMF: Guilty as Charged," *Envio: The Monthly Magazine of Analysis on Central America*, Universidad Centroamericana, Managua, Nicaragua, December 1994, p. 34.
   This "verdict" was issued by the 1994 session of the Permanent Peoples' Tribunal to follow up a previous commitment to evaluate IMF and World Bank policies with respect to international law and the right to self-determination.

20. John Dillon, Ecumenical Coalition for Economic Justice, *Turning the Tide: Confronting the Money Traders*, Ottawa: Canadian Centre for Policy Alternatives, 1997. The quotations that follow can be found within pp. 1-9.

21. *Ibid.*, pp. 8, 9.

22. Mike Moore, "Shackling the Genie," editorial in *The Bulletin of the Atomic Scientists*, March/April 1996, p. 2.

23. Mike Moore, "Midnight Never Came," in *The Bulletin of the Atomic Scientists*, November/ December 1995, pp. 16-27.

24. Mike Moore, "Behind the Clock Move," in *The Bulletin of the Atomic Scientists*, March/April 1996, pp. 17-23. The "Board Statement" is on page 21.

25. David Orchard, "Trash Candu: Unsafe At Any Depth" in *Common Ground*, February 1997, p. 42.

26. David Suzuki, Chair of The David Suzuki Foundation, in a public letter with a "WARNING." "It's the key issue of this century" but "Canadian politicians are refusing to take serious action on Climate Change because they think Canadians like you don't care!" February 1997.

27. (a) Chakravarthi Raghavan, "Southern lives are cheaper, say climate change economists" in *Third World Resurgence* No. 64, December 1995.
    "A recent meeting of the Intergovernmental Panel on Climate Change in Montreal has rejected and castigated the methodology employed by one of its working groups to assess the monetary damage caused by global warming."

    (b) Copy of an eight-page fax about a paper entitled, "The Unequal Use of the Global Commons" by Working Group Three (WG3) of the Intergovernmental Panel on Climate Change for the Equity Workshop in Nairobi in July 1994.

28. Alan Ereira, producer for BBC, a feature-length version of the edited "Nature" program shown on PBS, "From the Heart of the World: The Elder Brothers' Warning." New York: Mystic Fire Video, 1991.

29. *The Hau de no sau nee Address to the Western World: A Basic Call to Consciousness*, Geneva, Switzerland, Autumn 1977. From the Iroquois Confederacy, Copyright 1978 by *Akwesasne Notes*, Mohawk Nation, Via Rooseveltown, New York, pp. 76-77.
    The Hau de no sau nee, the traditional Six Nations Council at Onandaga, New York, presented these position papers in Geneva at the request of the Non-Governmental Organizations of the United Nations in September, 1977. They "constitute an abbreviated analysis of Western history, and . . . call for a consciousness of the Sacred Web of Life in the Universe."
    "Our culture is based on a principle that directs us to constantly think about the welfare of seven generations into the future." p. 96.

30. A public appeal in 1981 for help in the Navajo people's struggle to hold on to the land they have inhabited for over 400 years: to urge that Congress repeal Public Law 93-531, "a tragic mistake based on erroneous information and advice and the lack of a true understanding of the situation. . . .The two sovereign peoples [Navajo and Hopi] should not be subject to the political manipulation of the US government and the energy companies." A copy is on file with the author.

31. (a) *People to People: Highlights from the Report of the Royal Commission on Aboriginal Peoples*, Minister of Supply and Services Canada, 1996.

(b) Jerry Mander, *In the Absence of the Sacred: The Failure of Technology and the Survival of the Indian Nations*, San Francisco: Sierra Club Books, 1991.

(c) *Aboriginal People of Canada and Their Environment*, Ottawa: National Indian Brotherhood, Revised Edition 1973.

(d) Bruce E. Johansen, *Forgotten Founders: How the American Indian Helped Shape Democracy*, Harvard and Boston, Massachusetts: The Harvard Common Press, a Gambit Book, 1982.

(e) Val Napoleon, a Cree, is an experienced worker with the Gitxsan First Nation around Hazelton, British Columbia. She is now studying at University of Victoria School of Law. In 1997 she made a presentation to the Restorative Justice Video Conference sponsored by the John Howard Society of B.C. The following excerpts are taken from her comments on "Restorative Justice: Considerations and Issues".

". . .I am horrified by the regressive political climate in B.C. I find it downright scary when I hear declarations about the need to be tougher on crime. And when I hear, just below the surface, calls for the death penalty. There is no distance here. This is about my family and people I love. . . .

"While I am obviously speaking from the perspective of a First Nations woman, the issues I've identified also affect other social sectors and mainstream society. . . .

"Finland has successfully insulated its criminal justice reform from partisan politics. . . .

"It's telling that Canada has twice as many prisoners per capita as Finland. In Canada, the system is now 15 percent over capacity. Rather than build more prisons, we need to find alternatives and we need to look at the high risk factors created by our social, economic, and political environments. Exploring alternatives requires intellectual courage, social imagination, and leadership. . . .

"We need a place to talk about our fears and where we learned them. We need to talk about the necessary work that must go on inside the relationship between victim and offender. We need to look at the effect of capital punishment and increased incarceration rates. How does this approach to justice shape our communities and our world? In short, we need to challenge all of our held assumptions about justice.

"The western justice culture is so pervasive that we begin to see it as 'normal'. . . .

"Every First Nation has a distinct culture that holds its ideology, social structure, and relationship to the environment. Because of recent history, these cultural systems are not readily apparent in all communities. In these situations, members of the judiciary and social services workers sometimes want to rush in and introduce approaches like circle sentencing because they've been successful elsewhere. This is a kind of 'community justice ready mix' that can further undermine people's identity and drive their own social structure into further obscurity.

"This brings cultural imperialism to a new level—among First Nations people as well—and it is just as damaging. . . .

"I hope that with self-government and the treaty [process], First Nations have an opportunity to build coherency by linking justice with social development, health, education, economics, and land and resource management. No one sector can create change—justice workers can't create change by themselves, neither can educators, social workers, or anyone else.

"In conclusion, there is an increased national consciousness about restorative justice, and a recognition by a number of provinces that the existing criminal justice system is actually worsening justice problems by undermining community responsibility for its own members. A number of provincial justice ministers, including B.C.'s, share an understanding that we are beyond the stage of 'pilots and plans,' and must move on to serious justice system reform. . . ."

(f) Rupert Ross, *Returning to the Teachings: Exploring Aboriginal Justice*, Toronto: Penguin Books, 1996.

(g) Walter Taylor, "The Relevance of the Indian Heritage to the Survival of Man" in *Exploration, Journal of the British Columbia Social Studies Teachers' Association*, Vol. 10, No. 1, Vancouver: B.C. Teachers' Federation, November 1969.

(h) Walter Taylor, "Diversity: The Medicine for Human Survival," Introduction for *Uncommon Controversy: Fishing Rights of the Muckleshoot, Puyallup, and Nisqually Indians*, A Report Prepared for the American Friends Service Committee, Seattle: University of Washington Press, 1970.

(i) Walt Taylor, "An Aboriginal and Ecological Conspiracy: The Life-Sustaining Turning Point in History," Victoria: *British Columbia Historical News*, Vol. 20, No. 4, Fall 1987, p. 3.

(j) George Clutesi, *Son of Raven, Son of Deer: Fables of the Tse-Shaht People*, Sidney, British Columbia: Gray's Publishing, 1967, pp. 9, 10.

(k) Stewart L. Udall, *The Quiet Crisis*, New York: Avon Books, 1963, p. 24.
      "...It is ironical that today the conservation movement finds itself turning back to ancient Indian land ideas, to the Indian understanding that we are not outside of nature, but of it. ....

      "In recent decades we have slowly come back to some of the truths that the Indians knew from the beginning: that unborn generations have a claim on the land equal to our own; that men need to learn from nature, to keep an ear to the earth, and to replenish their spirits in frequent contacts with animals and wild land. And most important of all, we are recovering a sense of reverence for the land. ...."

(l) Harold McCracken, *George Catlin and the Old Frontier: A Biography and Picture Gallery of the Dean of Indian Painters*, New York: Bonanza Books, 1959, p. 14.
      "... I love a people who have always made me welcome to the best they had ... who are honest without laws, who have no jails and no poorhouse ... who never take the name of God in vain ... who worship God without a Bible, and I believe that God loves them also ... who are free from religious animosities ... who have never raised a hand against me, or stolen my property, where there was no law to punish either ... who never fought a battle with white men except on their own ground ... and oh! how I love a people who don't live for the love of money." [From George Catlin, *Last Rambles Amongst the Indians of the Rocky Mountains and the Andes*, London, 1868, pp. 354-355.]

(m) The World Commission on Environment and Development (WCED), chaired by Norwegian Prime Minister, Dr. Gro Harlem Brundtland, *Our Common Future*, Toronto and elsewhere: Oxford University Press, 1987. In Chapter 4, "Population and Human Resources," see pages 114 to 116 under "Empowering Vulnerable Groups" from which the following quotes are excerpted:
      "... some communities—so-called indigenous or tribal peoples—remain isolated because of such factors as physical barriers to communication or marked differences in social and cultural practices. Such groups are found in North America, in Australia, in the Amazon Basin, in Central America, in the forests and hills of Asia, in the deserts of North Africa, and elsewhere.

      "The isolation of many such people has meant the preservation of a traditional way of life in close harmony with the natural environment. Their very survival depended on their ecological awareness and adaptation. ...

      "With the gradual advance of organized development into remote regions, these groups are becoming less isolated. Many live in areas rich in valuable natural resources that planners and 'developers' want to exploit and this exploitation disrupts the local environment so as to endanger traditional ways of life. The legal and institutional changes that accompany organized development add to such pressures. . . .

"Many groups become dispossessed and marginalized, and their traditional practices disappear. They become the victims of what could be described as cultural extinction.

"These communities are the repositories of vast accumulations of traditional knowledge and experience that links humanity with its ancient origins. Their disappearance is a loss for the larger society, which could learn a great deal from their traditional skills in sustainably managing very complex ecological systems. It is a terrible irony that as formal development reaches more deeply into rain forests, deserts, and other isolated environments, it tends to destroy the only cultures that have proved able to thrive in these environments. . . .

"The starting point for a just and humane policy for such groups is the recognition and protection of their traditional rights to land and other resources that sustain their way of life—rights they may define in terms that do not fit into standard legal systems. These groups' own institutions to regulate rights and obligations are crucial for maintaining the harmony with nature and the environmental awareness characteristic of the traditional way of life. Hence the recognition of traditional rights must go hand in hand with measures to protect the local institutions that enforce responsibility in resource use. And this recognition must also give local communities a decisive voice in the decisions about resource use in their areas. . . ."

(n) Peter Mathiessen, *Indian Country*, New York: Viking Press, 1984.
"Christopher Columbus, going ashore in the Antilles, was struck by the profound well-being of the island Arawak. ('There is not in the world a better nation. They love their neighbours as themselves, and their discourse is ever sweet and gentle.'. . .)

". . .three seamen of Drake's expedition . . ., left behind in Mexico in 1568, made their way unharmed all the way across the continent to Cape Breton Island, where they found passage home. The Indians strove to live honorably and responsibly as well as generously, and perhaps it was the very goodness of a 'heathen' people, so civilized in all meaningful ways, that was so disturbing to religious men who had to wrestle with the bestiality in their own natures. Since they intended to usurp the Indians' country, it must have soothed the Puritanical conscience to dismiss these open-hearted folk as 'wolves endewed with men's braines' (Roger Williams)—or 'hounds of hell,' in Cotton Mather's term—to be cleared from God's path as speedily as possible. Thus Captain John Mason, who led the villainous attack on a sleeping

Pequot village in 1634, exulted in 'burning them up in the fire of His wrath, and dunging the ground with their flesh. It was the Lord's doings, and marvelous in our eyes!'. . ." pp. 3,4.

(o) David Suzuki and Peter Knudtson, *Wisdom of the Elders: Sacred Native Stories of Nature*, New York: Bantam Books, 1993.

In "A Personal Foreword," David Suzuki wrote, ". . . As my understanding of indigenous people's deep attachment to place has grown, I am impelled to support many groups seeking allies to protect their land. If biodiversity and ecosystem integrity are critical to salvaging some of the skin of life on earth, then every successful fight to protect the land of indigenous peoples is a victory for all of humanity and other living things. More and more people from dominant Western cultures are recognizing this and forming alliances with indigenous peoples. . . .

"The ecological impact of industrial civilization and the sheer weight of human numbers is now global and is changing the biosphere with frightening speed. It is clear that major problems such as global warming, ozone depletion, species extinction, and worldwide toxic pollution will not be solved in the long run by perpetuating the current worldview and applying Band-Aids such as tax levies, greater efficiency, and recycling. Knowledge gained through science is unique and profound, yet also extremely limited. Not only does the Newtonian worldview fail to comprehend the complexity of life on earth, we have barely begun to understand its dimensions.

"We need a radically different way of relating ourselves to the support systems of the planet. My experiences with aboriginal peoples have convinced me, both as a scientist and as an environmentalist, of the power and relevance of their knowledge and worldview in a time of imminent global ecocatastrophe. . . ."

With co-author, Peter Knudtson, he wrote: "Our shared perceptions and fundamental belief in the validity and power of aboriginal notions of the sacredness of Nature have produced this book." pp. xlii-xliv.

危机 CHAPTER 2

Allowing Two Colossal Problems to Solve Each Other

> Supply and Demand works only when people with demands can afford their supplies.
> —Common understanding

Many years ago I paid a visit to the Bronx Zoo in New York. My attention was drawn immediately to one corner far away from me where huge vertical bars on a special cage protected observers from the animal inside. In bright red letters a large sign warned me, even from a distance, that the caged specimen was "THE MOST DANGEROUS ANIMAL ON EARTH." On moving closer, however, all I could see behind those heavy bars was my own self reflected in a mirror.

At this turn of the millennium all life which depends on the health of Mother Earth is at risk. The main cause of this unprecedented danger is the behaviour of our own human species, including myself, especially during the twentieth century.

Chapter 1 provided compelling evidence of the extent and imminence of this danger. The warning signals keep telling us to stop, look, and listen while we translate our awareness of extreme danger into effective action appropriate to the severity of our predicament.

First problem

Global and regional *problem number one* is the urgent need to employ more people in actually doing all the work required to end our "drift toward unparalleled catastrophe" and to open the way for our transition to sustainable living. Most important of all, we need to discover or possibly even invent the best ways to cultivate some absolutely necessary changes in our "modes of thinking." We have to make full use now of everyone's imagination and collaboration.

Second problem

Global and regional *problem number two* is high unemployment together with wasteful underemployment. A huge number of people in Canada and even more around the world cannot earn a living for themselves and their families because public and private enterprises do not offer enough paid work for everyone.

Every human being on earth needs to be needed, almost as much as a person needs food, water, and shelter. In our present highly competitive "global economy," dedicated to maximizing private profits and trying to reduce deficits by severely "downsizing" both public and private employment, many millions of world citizens are being told that their work is not needed, that they really have no value in our globalized society. In this situation it is understandable that so many people feel worthless.

Unemployment and underemployment are unhealthy, unaffordable, and actually unnecessary. With all the wealth in this world, and such a vast amount of challenging and urgently needed work still ahead of us, both unemployment and underemployment are not only intolerable, they are utterly inexcusable.

A perfect fit

It is obvious that the pressing need for more workers and high unemployment are two serious problems which fit together so well that each represents a perfect solution to the other. What will it take to achieve a blessed marriage between them?

I think it will take an action plan: first, to identify the work that must be done; second, to develop effective ways to pay for it; and then to begin actually doing it.

In order to achieve a sustainable future, great changes are needed in almost every aspect of life from agriculture, fishing, mining, and forestry to health, economics, education, and human rights. This need for change provides many opportunities right in front of us for non-profit but high-benefit work. Other new opportunities have yet to be imagined.

To respond effectively to so many daunting challenges and haunting opportunities will require public dedication comparable to the *patriotic participation* which flourishes in time of war, whenever one's fatherland is threatened. Now that the whole Earth, the motherland, is in serious danger, all people everywhere must find ways to do whatever work is necessary to protect this Mother on whom all life depends. Since we have to change "our modes of thinking," an appropriate new mode might be called *matriotic participation* in protecting Mother Earth, the only home we have.

We must, in fact, WAGE PEACE FOR A LIVING. That is the action plan proposed in this book.

In the old days when war often seemed justifiable and necessary to most people, a standard patriotic slogan advised, "If you want peace, prepare for war." Now that we can see war more clearly as an obvious contributor to the risk of "unparalleled catastrophe," the University for Peace in Costa Rica displays a revised slogan, more appropriate to our modern struggle for survival into the twenty-first century and the next millennium: "If you want peace, prepare for peace."

Of course genuine peace implies much more than the mere absence of war. Genuine peace requires respect for the earth and all its life. It means living within the planet's carrying capacity, its remarkable but nevertheless finite ability to regenerate its natural resources and assimilate waste. Genuine peace calls for sharing the wealth with more reasonable fairness and sharing responsibility for sustaining the health of all life for our own and future generations.

The alternative to undertaking this challenging struggle to change our modes of thinking is grim: "unparalleled catastrophe."

The possible benefits of an all-out, total effort to wage peace will far exceed the costs. While achieving virtually full employment, those who wage peace successfully will also encourage health and cooperative living for life on earth during the next seven generations.

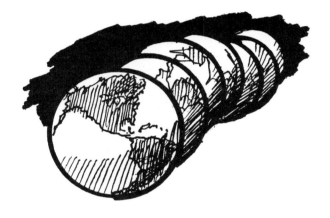

. . .health and cooperative living for life on earth during the next seven generations.

危机 CHAPTER 3

An Action Plan:
Waging Peace for a Living

> Surely if we can produce in such abundance in order to destroy our enemies, we can produce in equal abundance in order to provide food, clothing and shelter for our children. If we can keep people employed for the purpose of destroying human life, surely we can keep them employed for the purpose of enriching and enhancing human life.
>
> —Tommy Douglas, 1945

When world war threatens, an emergency is declared. When an evil enemy, like the Nazis in the 1930s and 1940s, commits outrageous atrocities and presents a military threat to the lives, property, and future of one's country and allies, an emergency is declared. When people suffer enormous damage by flood, fire, drought, famine, earthquake, hurricane, oil spill, or volcano, the affected region is called a disaster zone, and an emergency is declared.

Whatever it takes to win the war against Man or Nature will be spent without question, regardless of the total expense in dollars, resources, research, manpower, lost lives, displaced persons, and environmental devastation. Meat, sugar, and gasoline are rationed, unnecessary civilian production is terminated, dykes are built, or bomb shelters constructed.

People volunteer or are conscripted for work and military service. Soldiers and civilians undergo accelerated training programs in how to plan, organize themselves, respond to air-raid warnings, and do whatever else survival of the group may require. Total, all-out war imposes sacrificial conditions on everyone, and almost everyone accepts the hardships "for the duration."

Now is the time for a total, all-out commitment to waging peace for the duration of our global emergency. But who ever heard of "waging peace?" What is that? Why wage peace?

Well, the "drift toward unparalleled catastrophe" that worried Albert Einstein half a century ago has not gone away. The danger to life on earth has actually worsened so much that our whole planet should now be declared a disaster zone. Since the military-corporate complex has gained control over most government decisions, we cannot expect political leaders to provide emergency funding for such a collossal disaster zone—or even to recognize the unprecedented dangers we face and the extraordinary opportunities available now, at last, to make genuine progress toward peace with justice. Therefore, we, the people, will have to understand and spread the word about our global situation.

What will it really take for us to make the absolutely necessary changes in "our modes of thinking?"

To answer this question, some helpful advice came along with the dire warnings presented in Chapter 1. We must "abandon limited selfish interests to the realization of a common need" according to the 1970 message to our billions of neighbours from thousands of scientists around the world.[1] In 1991 the Blue Planet Group declared that we must now "recognize that we cannot go on as before, and embark immediately and deliberately upon a bold course of global ecological sustainability" that calls for nothing less than "an unparalleled revolution in our way of thinking about our future."[2]

The David Suzuki Foundation reported that "we are learning . . . that the earth's resources are not limitless, the economy cannot continue to grow forever, and we are part of Nature, not superior to it."[3] How shall we turn such wisdom that we have been learning into responsible action? If we take the 1992 *World Scientists' Warning to Humanity* seriously, we shall do everything possible to avoid the threatening deluge of "vast human misery" and to defend "our global home on this planet" against becoming "irretrievably mutilated." What specific work must we do now in order to bring about the essential "great change in our stewardship of the earth and the life on it?"[4]

Fundamental change

For life to persist and thrive in the twenty-first century we who now share this planet have both an obligation and an opportunity to take a quantum leap beyond our twentieth century modes of thinking.

Just to illustrate the magnitude of these necessary changes, consider two familiar areas of work: economics and ecology. It will require a huge amount of challenging new work to enable us to change our customary way of thinking about economics and ecology as two separate and often competing fields of work. We must begin to understand them as one intimately interconnected, cooperative approach to planning and working in the twenty-first century. Ecological economics must become a significant part of our new modes of thinking.[5] (For a more detailed discussion of ecological economics, see Chapter 10.]

Facilitating other needed paradigm shifts will also keep many people employed for some time to come. One prevailing paradigm assumes incorrectly that most non-profit work must necessarily be done by volunteers. Now is the time to recognize that waging peace effectively, like waging war, cannot depend on volunteers alone.

Removing unnecessary obstacles

Two widespread misconceptions now dominate much thinking in Canada and elsewhere and control most government budgets and policies. The first is that there is no longer enough work for everyone. According to some analysts, we have "advanced" so far we have finally come to "the end of work".[6]

The second misconception, based on heavy pressure to reduce deficits, cut taxes, and downsize government expenditures and services, maintains that we simply cannot afford to pay for significant non-profit work, even work that absolutely must be done to sustain life on this planet.

Evidence to the contrary in each case is compelling.

In the unprecedented predicament of Mother Earth and her life as we approach a new century and the next millennium, there is plenty of urgently needed work to keep everyone on this planet fully employed for the foreseeable future. Some of that work can turn a profit and pay its own way, but much of it is non-profit work that will require substantial financial support. The action plan in this book is mainly concerned with work that is essential, but not financially profitable.

Furthermore, there is sufficient wealth on our good earth to allow those who actually do all this necessary work to earn an adequate income for themselves and their families.

To connect all this important work with appropriately educated workers and enough money to support them will require an extraordinary investment in talent, dedication, and imagination by our whole society. To get over the hurdles and around the obstacles ahead some preparation is in order.

A way forward

The first task suggested for WAGING PEACE FOR A LIVING will be to build two necessary instruments that communities, regions, and/or nations can use to allow each place to carry out its own necessary local work, and also to undertake its full share of the global work required for a transition to sustainable ways of living and earning a living. These two essential instruments are:

• a WORK INVENTORY—what actually needs to be done, and

• a FINANCIAL SUPPORT INVENTORY—ways to pay for all that work.

This action plan will unfold in three phases in order to respond adequately to the unprecedented challenges we face and to take full advantage of the opportunities we shall open up.

The first phase of WAGING PEACE FOR A LIVING will be a time for research, at least a year, to prepare a workable first draft of the two necessary inventories.

The second phase will be five years devoted to demonstration projects in several experimental communities or regions to test the best ways of using these instruments to get high priority, low impact work underway. In addition to the local and global benefits expected as a result of doing all this valuable work, one priceless by-product for each demonstration region will be virtually full employment.

In the third phase of WAGING PEACE FOR A LIVING an information campaign across Canada and around the world will make it possible for interested communities everywhere to adopt and use these two instruments—or to adapt them to each region's own distinctive circumstances and cultures.

For this effort to succeed in Canada and worldwide, the global FINANCIAL SUPPORT INVENTORY for waging peace will have to continue growing, possibly even to the extent of matching what the world now spends for military purposes, including waging war.

How this plan could work

Just to illustrate how this proposed action plan might look in a region where unemployment is high and resources are limited, consider any of the many communities where a long established industry has moved away or closed, or a mine has shut down, or logging or fishing has been severely restricted in an effort to conserve depleted resources.

With the WORK INVENTORY in front of them, people in each interested region will first decide together what local work really needs to be done for their own people. They will also study the WORK INVENTORY to discover what other work is urgently needed for the survival and health of the whole planet and to reduce the dangerously growing gap between extreme wealth and utter poverty. They will think together about how they can do their share of the necessary global work as well as the work required in their own home region.

Instead of selecting only work that seems financially affordable, profitable, or otherwise "realistic" and "doable," the community thinkers will dare to take on work projects that are so absolutely necessary that responsible citizens *cannot afford to leave them undone*, regardless of cost.

That bold approach will make it possible for society to take the essential quantum leap from our present perilous predicament to a promising future for our own and the next seven generations.

With the FINANCIAL SUPPORT INVENTORY on the table next to the WORK INVENTORY, these bold and daring work plans that have been identified as absolutely necessary will also become affordable and realistic.

With the FINANCIAL SUPPORT *INVENTORY on the table next to the* WORK INVENTORY. . .

Notes

1. *Op. cit.*, Chapter 1, Note 11.

2. *Op. cit.*, Chapter 1, Note 12.

3. *Op. cit.*, Chapter 1, Note 13.

4. *Op. cit.*, Chapter 1, Note 14.

5. Herman E. Daly, "From empty-world economics to full-world economics: Recognizing an historical turning point in economic development," Chapter 2, pp. 29-38 in *Environmentally Sustainable Economic Development: Building on Brundtland*, edited by Robert Goodland, Herman Daly, Salah El Serafy and Bernd von Droste, Paris: UNESCO (United Nations Educational, Scientific and Cultural Organization), 1991.

   Chapter 1 by Robert Goodland, "The case that the world has reached limits: More precisely that current throughput growth in the global economy cannot be sustained," pp. 15-27.

6. (a) Jeremy Rifkin, *The End of Work: The Decline of the Global Labour Force and the Dawn of the Post-Market Era*, New York: G. P. Putnam's Sons, 1995.

   (b) Stanley Aronowitz and William Di Fazio, *The Jobless Future: Sci-Tech and the Dogma of Work*, Minneapolis: University of Minnesota Press, 1994.

   (c) Jennifer Wells, "Jobs: Government cuts and corporate layoffs create a national mood of insecurity" in *Maclean's*, March 11, 1996.

   (d) Roy Culpepper, President, North-South Institute, "Anti-employment bias" in *CCPA Monitor*, Ottawa: Canadian Centre for Policy Alternatives, July/August 1996.
   " . . . Both monetary and fiscal policy are now biased against full employment—monetary policy being used to counteract any inflation-inducing surge in employment, and fiscal policy being obsessed with massive expenditure reduction. The real purpose of the recent G7 Jobs Summit in Lille was to allow G7 governments to reaffirm their anti-inflation, anti-full-employment stance, and to deflate any expectation of better economic news."

The Upholders of Justice—"You were hungry . . . you were hungry . . . that's no excuse . . . I myself am hungry nearly every day but that doesn't make me steal!"

—*Honoré Daumier, French caricaturist (1808-1879)*

危机 CHAPTER 4

An Invitation to NGO Initiative

> If you have come to help me you are wasting your time.
> But if you have come because your liberation is bound
> up with mine, then let us work together.
> —Lilla Watson, an Australian
> Aboriginal woman

How can our society begin the enormous amount of cooperative effort required for our tremendous transition from despair to hope? We have to make a fundamental change away from our business-as-usual, downstream drift toward unparalleled catastrophe and into an upstream struggle for our very survival. Like salmon preparing to jump a waterfall, we need a running start for our elevation to new modes of thinking and effective ways of doing all the work required for our future existence.

The WAGING PEACE FOR A LIVING proposal belongs to everyone who is concerned. Some enthusiastic individual, group, or coalition may adopt it as a rough draft on which to base a workable plan ready for funding and action. The particular ideas offered in this book might also be worth considering on their own individual merits.

Many excellent non-governmental organizations (NGOs) are already taking action in their own special fields to heal some of our deep, twentieth century wounds and to make progress toward a sustainable future.

However, if several of these organizations were to cooperate specifically to understand our interconnected, unprecedented global problems more completely and explore appropriate ways to respond to them, the ideas they could produce would certainly enhance the waging peace proposal and might even supplant it with a more advanced plan.

I believe that it will take this combination of the talents of a few NGOs dedicated to a major common purpose to accomplish miracles which might otherwise seem utterly impossible. A coalition of NGOs could begin to open the way for our urgently needed quantum leap toward virtually full employment all over the world doing meaningful work for the continuing survival of life on earth.

A very wise recommendation comes to mind here. I confess that I probably advocate this suggestion a little more often than I manage to practice it:

> You can accomplish almost anything if you don't mind
> who gets the credit.
> ——A. Nonymous

How could such collaboration begin?

Since everything in life is somehow connected to everything else, an NGO coalition for survival will benefit from the participation of as many organizations as possible, especially because their individual interests cover so many different but interrelated fields of work.

The effort could begin, however, with representatives of only a few interested NGOs meeting together. Even one or two NGOs could plan together the best ways to attract other groups to participate in a cooperative endeavour which could do wonders for the world and at the same time expand and strengthen the valuable work that each organization is already doing.

NGOs and the Work Inventory

In their annual appeals, most NGOs summarize their year of crucial accomplishments, and suggest that an increase in financial support would allow them to undertake promising new work and extend their old work to a larger area to serve more needs. They know from their own experience that a huge amount of desperately needed work is not being done right now for lack of adequate resources.

For example, Physicians for Global Survival (PGS) recently reported on that organization's work for nuclear weapons abolition, the landmines ban, support for landmine survivors, assistance to students, and other initiatives. Some of its ambitious concerns are: preventing war, participating in the International Physicians for the Prevention of Nuclear War, social justice (respecting human rights), health, and a sustainable world.

Obviously, PGS must have a long list of work projects they consider necessary, but they lack the means to tackle them at this time. In cooperation with other NGOs, PGS could contribute significantly to a global list of work that must be undertaken soon for survival. I have called this list of needed projects the WORK INVENTORY.

To suggest just a few other examples of relevant NGOs, among many hundreds, consider Inter Pares for one, a non-profit international development agency. Inter-Pares works overseas and in Canada in support of self-help development groups, and in the promotion of understanding about the causes, effects, and alleviation of underdevelopment and poverty.

One Inter Pares *Bulletin* focused on a vast global network of hope, determination, and action for change—what they like to call an "open conspiracy"—because this informal network seeks collective action to create fundamental social change.

Consider also Peacefund Canada, which supported in one year more than thirty individuals and organizations involved in innovative peace education projects in Africa, Asia/Pacific, India and Pakistan, Europe and the Middle East, Latin America, and North America.

In addition to providing direct support to groups in areas of acute conflict, Peacefund Canada has served as the lead agency of an ad hoc group of NGOs in Canada which seeks to collaborate with NGOs in war zones in order to build peace. Those in Canada have included the Canadian Council for International Cooperation,

United Church of Canada, Mennonite Central Committee, Médecins Sans Frontières, International Development Research Centre, Physicians for Global Survival, Canadian Peacebuilding Coordinating Committee, and Project Ploughshares.

As a third example, I shall mention briefly The David Suzuki Foundation which sponsors excellent scientific research, public education, and action leadership for living in balance with the rest of the planet within limits set by Nature instead of our economic, political, and industrial priorities. Although well known internationally for publicizing thoroughly documented evidence that our planet and its life are in terrible danger, the Foundation is equally involved in *Finding Solutions*, the title of its newsletter.[1]

All NGOs are extremely busy with the work at hand, but they know there is much more to be done. It may seem difficult, however, if not impossible, for them to spare any staff or time for WAGING PEACE FOR A LIVING, no matter how well the need is appreciated.

For that reason I propose that each interested NGO prepare a rough estimate of how much extra financial support it will need in order to provide the necessary time and staff to participate in the initial steps toward an effective, cooperative action plan for the survival of life on earth. I believe the very first steps will be for a small group of NGO representatives to reach a consensus on the most promising action plan they can imagine and then to work together on the best possible ways to implement it.

As soon as these cost estimates for participation in the first steps are known, I am confident that a number of enthusiastic advocates will quickly find ways to raise sufficient funds to cover them.

In Appendix II readers will find a more detailed explanation for my estimated cost of $500,000 for the next step—preparing in one year the first drafts for a WORK INVENTORY and a FINANCIAL SUPPORT INVENTORY.

The NGOs will not have to carry out all by themselves this year of research to produce the two inventories, but each one will be able to contribute significantly to the WORK INVENTORY from its own experience and knowledge of important work that is not being done.

The WORK INVENTORY must include all the work required to respond effectively to the many dire warnings we have received about the unprecedented dangers that we and other life on earth must now face. In order to complete such a comprehensive list of work to be done, NGOs and other participants will have to overcome their natural tendency to be "reasonable" and "realistic." As it is in world wars, the threats to our future are beyond "reasonable" and it is most unrealistic to allow them to continue without taking bold action to defend the planet and its life.

NGOs and the Financial Support Inventory

In order to pay for all the work ahead of us it will be necessary to invent some new ways to obtain sufficient contributions for a very substantial global fund. To wage peace and restore health to our planet may require as much as the world now spends to prepare for and wage war, about $1 trillion per year.

A large part of that Trillion Dollars-Per-Year Fund will go to NGOs to strengthen their resource base and extend the work they are already doing in order to accomplish the work compiled in the WORK INVENTORY. All around the world, NGOs have earned a fine public reputation for integrity and successful efforts to overcome formidable obstacles. They have many years of experience handling delicate situations, respecting cultural differences, and confronting difficult and sometimes seemingly hopeless challenges. NGO employees and volunteers have demonstrated the concern, the imagination, the dedication, and the talent required for undertaking a bold and responsible action plan for survival.

In addition to their key role in developing the inventories, NGOs will be needed in the crucial task of putting together a group of highly respected and trusted world citizens to be responsible for fair and effective methods of distributing funds and making sure that essential work is done and done well.

Unprecedented cooperative fund-raising

The primary task of this book is to propose a way to identify the actual work required for survival of our own and future generations of life on earth. I shall discuss that in more detail in Chapter 5.

However, the most severe critics of WAGING PEACE FOR A LIVING will probably ask, "Where will you ever find the money for such an outrageously expensive plan? Isn't it obvious that we can never afford any trillion dollars per year? Can't you see that WAGING PEACE FOR A LIVING is only an idle dream with no realistic financial base?"

For a sustainable future I believe the world's people will respond to a cooperative drive for as much as $1 trillion per year for as many years as necessary. The turn of the millennium is a most appropriate time to launch an unprecedented action, at the end of a century of astounding technological achievement, but also of unprecedented assault on the earth and its life.

Chapter 6 will explore some promising but rarely mentioned benefits of cooperation among NGOs. Working together in a major cooperative fund-raising campaign will actually provide more funds for each organization than competing separately for financial support.

At the same time, however, the collective power of collaborating NGOs will significantly strengthen the initial waging peace project: to identify the most important work to be done and to plan how to raise the substantial core funding required for survival.

NGOs and the well-being of future generations

After living through most of the amazing achievements and the devastating horrors of the twentieth century, I am taking a good, hard look at future prospects for our own and the next seven generations of life on earth. My view is not seen through any rose-coloured glasses, but rather through the realistic lens of unfettered determination and unquenchable hope: the many reports and appeal letters I receive from NGOs. Through them I can foresee a future which will become increasingly possible as the organizations grow stronger.

I can foresee that it is the NGOs that have the collective potential to reverse our current downward spiral. That reversal will begin when even a few NGOs adopt a cooperative approach to identifying the work that needs to be done for survival, and inventing the best ways to provide sufficient funds to allow those who do all this work to earn a living.

That is our goal: for virtually all the people on earth to become fully employed doing this very important work. Then most of the world's tough problems will begin to yield to this exciting outbreak of changing modes of thinking from bottom-line competition to a far more effective, all-out spirit of cooperation—above the bottom-line, right up to the pinnacle of long-range survival and well-being for life on earth.

. . . right up to the pinnacle of long-range survival . . .

Notes

1. One of the many significant publications of the David Suzuki Foundation
    in Vancouver is *Living Within Our Means: The Foundations of Sustainability* by
    Dr. John Robinson and Caroline Van Bers, published in March 1996. Dr.
    Robinson is Director of the Sustainable Development Research Institute,
    University of British Columbia; Caroline Van Bers is an environmental
    consultant with Dovetail Consulting in Vancouver.

危机 CHAPTER 5

Building the WORK INVENTORY

> When something so fundamental as water becomes
> scarce, only fundamental responses will suffice.
> —*State of the World 1990*

In preparing to wage peace, the first requirement will be to identify the work that must be done for society to make the necessary changes to restore health to our planet and well-being to our own and future generations of life on earth. One good research team will produce a useful, first draft WORK INVENTORY in one year, a catalogue of high priority work for regional and global agenda.

The second requirement will be to identify effective ways to pay for all that necessary work, especially since much of it will be non-profit work. A second good research team will begin at the same time as the first to prepare a useful, first draft FINANCIAL SUPPORT INVENTORY in one year.

Both research projects will run simultaneously, but I discuss the WORK INVENTORY first because our main concern is to get urgently needed work underway as soon as possible. I want to respond in this chapter to the mistaken view that there is no longer enough work for everyone.

Only a few pages further on, in Chapter 6, I shall examine the other question, equally essential for getting the work done, "How in the world do you think we could ever find the money to pay for all that work?" By postponing any question of affordability to

Chapter 6, we can freely explore here work that is so necessary that we cannot afford to leave it undone regardless of cost.

Fields of work toward a sustainable society

Although it may disappoint some readers, this book cannot supply any catalogue of work that needs to be done. The actual WORK INVENTORY must be prepared by an able, forward-thinking research team. In this chapter, however, I shall present evidence that there is, in fact, plenty of urgently needed work to keep everyone employed.

Contrary to the title of an excellent recent book by Jeremy Rifkin, *The End of Work* [1], there is, in fact, *no* end of work! I do agree with Rifkin and others that we are experiencing a severe and persistent downsizing of the kind of full-time, career work that has been paid for in the past by public agencies and private corporations. That type of work provided regular income and benefits for professionals and other employed workers. Unfortunately many of those employees have now either lost jobs which they thought were secure or they continue working, maybe part-time, but with reduced income and benefits as well as much more anxiety about their future.

In every familiar field of work there are opportunities to make changes that will help to overcome the great dangers we face and encourage beneficial alternatives. I shall discuss some of these opportunities one by one, but it is important to acknowledge that all fields of work are intimately interrelated, and each one is capable of either facilitating or obstructing the changes needed in other fields.

In recent decades, competition has taken first place among the key rules for success in business. Given our perilous regional and global predicament, sustainable success will now depend increasingly on our willingness and ability to switch our emphasis to mutual appreciation, respect, reconciliation, collaboration, and cooperation regionally and globally. Struggling to achieve this transition from excessive competition to increasing cooperation is one way to describe the process of waging peace.

What is all this urgently needed work?

The order in which I have placed the following fields of work does not imply any ranking of importance. Keep in mind that every field of work is significant and that all fields of work are interconnected.

HUMAN RIGHTS. Inhuman wrongs have overwhelmed people in the twentieth century so completely that our numbed feelings make it difficult even to hear new reports, much less take adequate and appropriate action in response.

Many NGOs are doing magnificent work in reporting savage human rights violations and creating opportunities for concerned citizens to protest wrongs and promote rights. However, the continuing need far exceeds the resources available. Most of the good work is being done by volunteers now, but to accomplish adequate improvements will require a substantial increase in resources, including the number of employees able to earn a living in the work of promoting human rights.

Work is needed to address regional and global poverty and its consequences, including starvation and malnutrition, ill health, dependency, unsafe water, homelessness, and powerlessness.

To narrow significantly the widening chasm between poor and rich people, creative work carried on by such NGOs as Canada's National Anti-Poverty Organization will require a substantial increase in the number of competent, paid workers. They have to contend with heavily financed, professional campaigns to downsize social safety nets, reduce taxes, allow loans from the World Bank and the International Monetary Fund only at the price of complying with requirements for structural adjustments (which impose an outrageous burden on poor people while further enriching the already affluent.)

ENVIRONMENT. The response of most nations, including wealthy industrial countries, has been far from adequate to satisfy the substantial requirements for survival and sustainability that have been presented at extraordinary international conferences and in powerful warnings signed by many hundreds of the world's leading scientists and other distinguished and concerned thinkers.

Just a few brief comments should be sufficient to illustrate the enormous amount of urgently needed work required to restore health to our regional and global environment and protect it for future generations.

In addition to the substantial but insufficient work now being done, very often by volunteers in NGOs, the world desperately needs a massive increase in paid work opportunities for men and women who have been getting good training in environmental studies, but too often find limited or no opportunities to earn a living in their chosen field of work.

For ecosystem problems, we need many more employees to address deforestation, global warming, fossil fuel burning, acid rain, ozone layer depletion, poisoning by radioactivity, pesticides, herbicides and emissions.

For ecosystem solutions, we need skilled, imaginative, forward-thinking employees to devise and undertake bold actions to restore healthy conditions for water, air, soil, biological diversity, and ozone protection in the stratosphere.

As one example, consider that safe water is an absolute necessity for everyone. Non-profit projects will need many good workers to construct new water and sewage facilities where needed and maintain old systems, improve the conservation of water, prevent pollution, and establish ecological priorities for the uses of water.

We need workers for much more effective waste management. In this field as in many others, we already know some very good solutions, but political decision makers claim that we cannot afford them. In the long run, however, future disasters will cost many billions of dollars and years of misery unless we begin soon to employ well trained and inventive people to help recycle or compost useful waste and safely dispose of hazardous waste.

ECOLOGICAL ECONOMICS. Ecological economics is not yet widely understood or even well known. Ecological economics will necessarily differ from established economics which continues now to promote maximum private profit at a totally unacceptable public cost to human rights, planet earth, and the very existence of future generations of people and other living things.

Ecological economist Herman E. Daly together with Kenneth N. Townsend published *Valuing the Earth: Economics, Ecology, Ethics* in 1993.[2] For a brief explanation of ecological economics I have borrowed some bare essentials of the concept from Herman Daly's chapter in a 1992 book, *Environmentally Sustainable Economic Development: Building on Brundtland.*[3] (Gro Harlem Brundtland of Norway chaired the World Commission on Environment and Development which published its report in 1987, *Our Common Future.*[4])

The title of Daly's chapter is "From empty-world economics to full-world economics: Recognizing an historical turning point in economic development." He points out that the world was indeed virtually "empty" in 1920, only 10 percent filled with people and our manufactured things. This small percentage of "fullness" has doubled, however, every 35 years—to 20 percent by 1955 and again to 40 percent by 1990. Many scientists believe that even 40 percent of the world filled with people and our man-made stuff exceeds the earth's carrying capacity. They think 40 percent may already go beyond the earth's remarkable, but nevertheless finite, ability to regenerate her natural resources and to assimilate waste.

By the year 2025, could the world actually become 80 percent full? And after that, unless some drastic changes intervene, what next? Can the earth possibly become 160 percent full of us?

Clearly, there is much work required for human beings even to recognize the dangerous obsolescence of our still prevailing "empty-world" economics, and then to make a paradigm switch in our modes of thinking in order to understand and begin to practice a new, unfamiliar, but much more realistic "full-world" economics.

To accomplish our urgently needed transition from the growthmania and corporate dominance of our currently prevailing economics to the steady-state, ecologically sensitive, cooperative qualities of ecological economics will require a quantum leap. It will take a substantial increase in the employment of appropriately educated ecological economists to help our society make necessary changes as the human population swells toward 14 billion or more in the twenty-first century. These changes in our socio-economic attitudes will be non-profit financially, and low impact environmentally, but of very high benefit for the planet and for our own and future generations of life on earth.

HEALTH AND SOCIAL SERVICES. There is a huge need around the world for more paid work in health and social services. Work to improve people's health is very closely related to much of the work that must be done in other fields such as human rights, environment, agriculture, population, and ecological economics. We can begin this discussion by paying attention to a well-established but little known analysis of the four main factors affecting human health and illness.

Among these four professionally recognized determinants of health, 10 percent depends on each person's physical environment; 15 percent is based on genetics, the genes that each person acquires at birth; 25 percent depends on medical care, more accurately described as "illness care."[5]

The remaining 50 percent, half of all the determinants of health, depends on the social and economic conditions in the life of each family or individual. Health or illness depends heavily on such factors as education, the quality of one's employment or the severity of one's unemployment, level of income, the distribution of income and wealth in the region where one lives, social supports when needed, and social justice.

People in higher income families are healthier than people with lower incomes for many reasons. They can afford better basic necessities, including nutrition, clothing, and shelter. They can also benefit from recreation and other healthy activities and choices above and beyond the bare essentials. Poverty, unemployment, and poor working conditions help to make people sick. People with adequate and rewarding employment can enjoy a greater sense of control over their lives, and this contributes to better health. To improve the overall health of a population, much non-profit work is needed to achieve more nearly full and meaningful employment and a healthier redistribution of wealth.

There is also much paid, non-profit work to be done providing social services for victims of abuse, crime, neglect, exploitation, unemployment, underemployment, and deprivation. Special needs children require skilled attention to enable them to grow up into capable, contributing adults. Families with comfortable incomes often find these services limited, but poor families face additional obstacles. In many situations the cost of special services for children will be more than offset by long-range savings for society.

We live in a time of savage downsizing in medical services and the consequent emergence of two-tiered health systems, both locally and globally. High quality medical care should be available to everyone. The delivery of such care to poorer people requires much work worldwide.

An exciting field of work in medicine and public health is rediscovering, developing, and providing effective alternatives to costly, sophisticated methods of treating illness. There is a great deal of research, education, and service delivery work to be done in this area.

Prevention of unnecessary illness makes good sense both socially and economically. The health need for paid, non-profit work in environmental protection is enormous, to establish univeral access to safe water, clean air, adequate sanitation, and decent, affordable housing.

Much profitable work is already underway in genetic engineering, but this field is in the hands of profit-oriented corporations. There is a clear need for non-profit work assessing the direction and implications of this work, and ensuring it is beneficial for our whole society.

More work is needed to develop and implement responsible plans for a sustainable global population. This includes ecological food production and better distribution to meet global human need.

Consider also the increasing rate of damage and even extinction imposed on other valuable life forms as human beings occupy and impinge on an increasing percentage of the earth's finite space above, below, and on the surface.

The human activity that most severely threatens the health of both people and planet earth is war. Corporations, nations, and individuals make money in the short run by developing and selling arms to anyone who will buy them, but the long-range cost of this military proliferation will burden and endanger our own and future generations far beyond our ability to pay. Eliminating the causes of war, and the urge to wage war, will keep many good workers employed for a long time to come. People who work in this high benefit, non-profit endeavour will deserve and earn their full pay.

EDUCATION. All the above fields of work will benefit from paid, non-profit work in education to help revolutionize our modes of thinking toward sustainable ways of living and earning a living.

Many NGOs are already providing impressive educational services for a beneficial transition from our customary dependence on waging war for alleged "security" to far more promising and equally exciting methods of waging peace. They need more people working full-time researching and teaching the attitudes, skills, and techniques for non-violent conflict resolution. There are already many such workers, but we need more.

Some aboriginal elders and other teachers around the world have especially appropriate qualifications from their many generations of amazing cultural survival after repeated attempts—whether well-intentioned or not—either to eliminate or to assimilate them.

To encourage the necessary changes in our modes of thinking we need integrated action. Paid, non-profit workers will combine research, education, counselling, spiritual/religious inspiration, ecological science, scholarship, journalism, art, drama, poetry, music and peer influence. Working together we can cultivate a total, all-out movement toward waging peace quite comparable in some ways to the dedicated commitment in past crises to waging total, all-out, sacrificial war "for the duration."

Organized military training and opportunities for field experience have been available for a long time. Both trainers and trainees have generally been paid for their services.

Now we need training and apprenticeships for waging peace, including a great variety of desirable skills. We can connect formal learning with life-long experience through work-study programmes and other apprenticeship arrangements for people to absorb the requirements and opportunities for living in a sustainable society. Training and experience will include arts, crafts, music, dance, and theatre, and will be available also for people with special needs and/or gifts.

Work is needed for media fairness and honest history: to stimulate opportunities for fair and accurate news reporting, including mutual and self-criticism in history; to provide regular reports on progress toward a sustainable society and obstacles yet to be overcome; to appreciate the modern relevance of the aboriginal heritage of wit, wisdom, spiritual quality, and experience of living with respect for all of nature—sharing everything, wasting nothing, and assuming responsibility, without question, for the well-being of the next seven generations.

SCIENCE, TECHNOLOGY, AND SECURITY. According to twentieth century modes of thinking, security has depended heavily on superior physical power. All over the world people have insisted on maintaining enough military and police strength to defend themselves and their interests against any and all enemies. That dedication to advanced military power has inspired and subsidized a large part of the world's astonishing achievements during the past century in science and technology.

Now is the time for new modes of thinking about security. According to foremost scientists in many countries, the whole world has actually become far less secure during the past half dozen decades while science and technology have accomplished enormous improvements in the deadliness of available weapons of mass destruction, from landmines to nuclear bombs.

From all that well-funded military science and technology some benefits do, of course, trickle down as useful contributions for meeting human and ecological needs. However, by changing our modes of thinking we will become able to inspire and subsidize research and development in science and technology that is specifically designed to provide sustainable security through preparing for and waging peace.

In the field of energy, for example, we have exhilarating opportunities for paid, non-profit work to expand rapidly the research, development, and implementation of ecological energy sources. Solar, wind and small stream hydro power are only a few of the many possibilities we have for escaping from too much dependence on nuclear energy, destructive hydro dams, and fossil fuels. Even among profit-oriented corporations we can already see great progress toward generating electricity from hydrogen and oxygen for vehicles and other engines without producing any harmful exhaust emission.

INFORMATION. Most of us are thoroughly informed by now that we are living in the so-called "Information Age." Indeed, many of us feel as though we receive a superabundance of "information" pouring over us like a deluge and into us like an involuntary, intravenous injection. Titillating reports about prominent people or allegations involving them in murder often dominate our front page news columns for weeks or even months. But how much of this information do we really need to hear or want to know?

At the same time, most North Americans, even though usually well-read, never once even heard of the *World Scientists' Warning to Humanity* [6] which was proclaimed in 1992 and signed by nearly 1700 of the world's most distinguished scientists from 71 different countries, including 104 Nobel Prize winners. As we saw in Chapter 1, but it bears repeating, that dire warning was not covered by CBC Radio until four years later in 1996; it was not published, let alone emphasized, in *The Globe and Mail* in Toronto; and it was rejected in the United States as "not newsworthy" by *The New York Times* and *The Washington Post!* [7]

Without question, much more work must be done in the information field just to sustain any hope whatsoever that humankind will respond before it is too late to the scientists' warning that "A great change in our stewardship of the earth and the life on it is required, if vast human misery is to be avoided and our global home on this planet is not to be irretrievably mutilated."

Daily newspapers regularly devote several pages to stocks and bonds and business reports. Radio and television spend time on these matters every day. Without apparent embarrassment they report that "the economy" is healthy even when (or because?) unemployment continues to devastate 10 percent of Canadians, while at least 20 percent of the world's people, including children, live in abject poverty.

We measure our economic "health" according to the size of our gross domestic product (GDP). Clifford Cobb, Ted Halstead and Jonathan Rowe wrote that the GDP "has become the very language of the nation's economic reportage and debate. . . . The GDP is simply a gross measure of market activity, of money changing hands. It makes no distinction whatsoever between the desirable and the undesirable, or costs and gains." To see what it really measures,

> The more the nation depletes its natural resources, the more the GDP increases. Pollution shows up twice as a gain: once when the chemical factory, say, produces it as a by-product, and again when billions of dollars are spent to clean up the toxic waste that results. Any medical bills arising from people's exposure to the pollution also show up as growth in the GDP.
>
> The GDP also ignores the distribution of income, so that enormous gains at the top appear as new bounty for all. It makes no distinction between the person in the secure high-tech job and the downsized white-collar worker who has to work at two jobs, if possible, for lower pay. . . .
>
> Our politicians, media and economic commentators dutifully continue to trumpet the GDP figures as information of great portent. But there is an urgent need for a new indicator of progress geared to the economy

> that actually exists—a Genuine Progress Indicator (GPI)
> that will include those important aspects of our
> economic lives that the GDP now ignores.[8]

Obviously, much information work will be required to demystify this dangerously distorted measure of our "economy."

Joyce Nelson underlined the need for such work when she wrote in *Sultans of Sleaze: Public Relations and the Media* :

> What is new in this century is a powerful system of
> mass media interlocked with a technological and
> economic agenda that now threatens the entire planet.
> The paradox we face is that our lifestyle of luxury and
> "progress"—promulgated through the media over this
> century—increasingly reveals itself to be the prescription
> for planetary suicide. Moreover, that media system . . .
> does not function to alert us to problems as soon as
> they are known, but instead is purposely controlled and
> used to keep us uninformed of critical problems, or
> misinformed about their causes and repercussions, and
> reassured that nothing needs to change.[9]

Why is all this necessary work not being done now?

There are two main reasons why absolutely necessary work is not already underway.

Reason number one: First, the public—of whom, by whom, and for whom democratic decisions should be made—the public is kept uninformed about the great problems of our day. A good friend of ours once opened a major conference in Northwest British Columbia by welcoming the participants to "our mushroom society." He explained, "We all know how mushrooms grow best—when they are kept in the dark and fed a lot of manure."[10]

In 1987 the Alternative News Indices Project (ANI) was sponsored at Carleton University in Ottawa, under the Centre for Communication, Culture and Society. ANI advocates reported that

> the nightly quotations of the day's tradings are little more
> than commercials for another way of life; a life where

you can count on the "invisible hand" to make money for you, a life that by definition has to remain a life of the few. . .

ANI did some research (back in 1986) to find out just who actually uses these daily reports on stocks and bonds, the standard news indices (SNI):

> A 1984 study report, published by the Toronto Stock Exchange, profiles Canadian stock holders. They are a small minority in the country: only 1,688,000 Canadians own shares. That's 9.4% of the adult population. . .While it is true that there are shareowners in virtually all income groups, incidence of share ownership increases dramatically with income. . . .
>
> Daily indices regarding stock trading, the price of gold, or the exchange rate of the Canadian dollar are largely irrelevant to [most] Canadians. . . .it is fair to say that, at best, a tenth of adult Canadians is concerned with the daily fluctuations of the markets and their indexical representation. . . .
>
> And so, the question remains: why do we continue to get standard news indices of a type we so obviously don't deserve?
>
> Any notion that SNI somehow tells us how 'healthy' the economy is, is highly questionable at best. Even the people working in the media were quick to point that out to us.[11]

The public will not become well informed about the true condition and direction of the economy so long as governments, industry and the media continue to conceal negative social, economic, and environmental trends behind frequent reports of a thriving GDP.

We desperately need a new, meaningful way of measuring economic health. The persistent old way—the GDP—responds only to the quantity of financial transactions regardless of whether they represent beneficial or harmful human activities. If scientists develop and successfully market a hydrogen fuel that produces no exhaust except water, the GDP goes up. However, the GDP still goes up when an airplane crashes or an oil spill pollutes a vast area of ocean.

We need what some have called a GPI, a Genuine Progress Indicator.[12] We have to elevate our public bottom line from maximum profits for a very few corporations and individuals up to the level of optimum health and well-being for all life, including Mother Earth herself. A GPI must go down, not up, when human activities are damaging to life or the environment. A GPI will go up only when human activities are beneficial to the well-being and future of life on earth.

As of this writing, I have seen no evidence of any switch from GDP to some form of GPI, although I understand that Statistics Canada at one time did consider developing a better way to measure economic health. Unfortunately, the GDP continues to rate an economy "healthy" if financial transactions are up even while unemployment stays high, the gap between rich and poor widens, and the global environment deteriorates.

Changing this will take a lot of high quality, non-profit work. Although the ANI project simply died for lack of sufficient financial support, something like it should be included in the WORK INVENTORY and funded through the FINANCIAL SUPPORT INVENTORY.

Reason number two: The second reason that so much urgently needed work is not being done now is that we don't even count non-profit work. We expect non-profit work to be done for free—or not at all. A huge amount of absolutely essential work is being done right now around the world—for free.

Marilyn Waring must be one of the best informed world experts on the vast amount of necessary work that gets done every day but does not count for anything in economic terms simply because it is unpaid, non-profit work for which no money changes hands. Most of this uncounted work is done by women who work very hard, but they themselves do not count any more in the world economy than their work does.

Marilyn Waring is a farmer. When she was elected as a very young but brilliant member of the New Zealand parliament, she wrote a book, *If Women Counted*.[13] In a Canadian National Film Board film called *Who's Counting?*[14] she revealed that she finally managed to penetrate the thick fog surrounding economics by mastering "the art of the dumb question." For example, when confronted with a pile of unintelligible economic reports on her parliamentary desk, she asked, "Is there any English to explain all this?" She flew to New York and spent time in Wall Street offices and libraries in her determination to uncover the truth behind economic reports that seem to be written in a deliberately obscure way to prevent ordinary people from understanding what is really going on.

Although much valuable non-profit work is already getting done without pay or recognition, much paid work will be necessary now to carry on Waring's attempt to shine enough clear light into mainstream economics to allow people to see through it and then begin to help change it. Economics must move away from its total focus on maximum profit and begin to pay increasing attention to the needs of people and protection for earth's finite resources. That improvement in economic analysis will benefit all people.

Even without the ANI and the proposed GPI, we already have many hundreds of forward-thinking scientific, economic, social, and cultural analysts and organizations publishing in the alternative press some realistic reports of our many interconnected global and regional problems.

In the mainstream media, however, it is harder to find the investigative journalism and critical analysis that people need. For some time now, a powerful combination of large corporations, financially elite think tanks, and other wealthy interests has dominated public policy and heavily influenced public opinion. We have been manipulated into believing that deficits must be reduced or eliminated; that governments are too big and spend too much; that environmental, labour, and human rights regulations are blocking economic progress; that some fairly high "natural" level of unemployment is necessary to prevent inflation; that the economy will boom when deficits and taxes come down allowing corporations and investors to engage in unfettered competition and flourish globally. Then, they say, we can depend on trickle-down benefits from all that prosperity to provide jobs and enable individuals to pay their own way for everything they need, including health, education, housing, and some kind of private insurance against hard times.

However, trickle-down has never actually happened. Instead, the affluent minority has been getting even wealthier as they pile still heavier burdens on the backs of the great majority of people who are not wealthy, and especially of those who are poor.

Many social deficits mean lots of work

One way to understand the extraordinary problems we face might be to think of them as social deficits, at least as worrisome as the fiscal deficit which has been dominating our news and controlling government policy and budgets for many years. A list of these social deficits may offer another way to think about the work ahead of us:

- the education deficit
- the employment deficit
- the deficit in awareness of relevant information
- the deficit in acknowledging earth's finite carrying capacity
- the deficit in understanding, developing, and practicing ecological economics
- the deficit in public awareness that some of us are overconsuming the earth's finite resources while others cannot even consume enough to support life
- the deficit in facing the implications of the human population explosion
- the deficit in recognizing and appreciating the modern relevance of aboriginal experience, wit, wisdom, survival expertise, and spiritual strength
- the human rights deficit
- the distribution deficit: the dangerously widening chasm between extreme wealth and utter poverty

- the public health and social services deficit
- the deficit in history presented from the viewpoint of oppressed and exploited people
- the deficit in essential priorities for science, technology, and security
- the deficit in political will to acknowledge danger and to take full advantage of opportunity

The WORK INVENTORY will provide a catalogue of the work required to transform these social deficits into stepping stones toward peace with justice.

... stepping stones toward peace with justice.

Notes

1. *Op. cit.*, Chapter 3, Note 6(a).

2. Herman E. Daly and Kenneth N. Townsend, Editors, *Valuing the Earth: Economics, Ecology, Ethics,* Cambridge, Massachusetts: The MIT Press, 1993.

3. *Op. cit.*, Chapter 3, Note 5.

4. *Op. cit.*, Chapter 1, Note 31 (m).

5. "Health Impact Assessment Guidelines, Part 2: Economic and Social Determinants of Health," Victoria: Population Health Resource Branch of the British Columbia Ministry of Health, 1995. The main source of this information is the Canadian Institute for Advanced Research in Toronto.

6. *Op. cit.*, Chapter 1, Note 14 (a).

7. *Op. cit.*, Chapter 1, Note 15.

8. Clifford Cobb, Ted Halstead, and Jonathan Rowe, "Why the GDP doesn't show economic reality," *CCPA Monitor*, Ottawa: Canadian Centre for Policy Alternatives, November 1995. Excerpted from an article in *Atlantic Monthly*, October, 1995.

9. Joyce Nelson, *Sultans of Sleaze: Public Relations and the Media*, Toronto: Between the Lines, 1989, p. 150.

10. John Jensen, at the Northwest Study Conference in Terrace, British Columbia, 1975. John Jensen is a union leader living in Terrace. Until recently he was President of the Northwest Study Conference Society.

11. Dr. Peter A. Bruck, *Alternative News Indices Project Update*, Number 1, Ottawa: April/May, 1987.
   Dr. Bruck launched the ANI project as Director of the Centre for Communication, Culture and Society at Carleton University in Ottawa. Unfortunately, the ANI project was terminated for lack of sufficient financial support. It is an excellent example of an urgently needed type of work that should be included in the WORK INVENTORY and funded through the FINANCIAL SUPPORT INVENTORY.

12. *Op. cit.*, Note 8.

13. Marilyn Waring, *If Women Counted: A New Feminist Economics*, New York: Harper SF, 1990.

14. Marilyn Waring, "*Who's Counting?*," National Film Board film, Montreal: 1995.
   Marilyn Waring clears away the dense fog of unnecessary complication that keeps any straightforward view of economics hidden from public scrutiny.

危机 CHAPTER 6

Immaculate Lucre: Building the
FINANCIAL SUPPORT INVENTORY

> We must invent a new economics, one that saves the
> capital stock and the life supporting air and water. There
> is plenty of money, plenty of work to be done, and
> workers to do it.
> —James F. Berry, 1987

In the *New Testament*, Timothy declared that "the love of money
is the root of all evil," and warned against being "greedy of filthy
lucre." The money assembled through the FINANCIAL SUPPORT
INVENTORY will be squeaky clean by its very nature because it will all
be used to pay for good work that is urgently needed.

The FINANCIAL SUPPORT INVENTORY will be prepared by a team of
inventive researchers. They may accept some of the ideas suggested
in this chapter, but they will inject their own ideas too. They may
even decide to replace this whole approach with a better plan.
Meanwhile, here is what I propose.

Cooperative investment for the next seven generations

The objective will be to develop and implement a cooperative plan
that will create and put to use an investment of $1 trillion per year
to foster full global employment doing all the necessary new work
and stimulating ecological ways of doing old work for the survival
and well-being of planet earth and its life for the next seven
generations.

This concept—that human beings carry a responsibility for the next seven generations—is borrowed from a very widespread aboriginal aphorism, ancient, but still vital. In their call for a consciousness of the "Sacred Web of Life in the Universe," the Hau de no sau nee explained that a fundamental principle in the Iroquois culture directs them to think constantly about the welfare of seven generations into the future.[1]

For more of us to adopt this responsible concern for the next 140 years would certainly be wise in our world which now spends $1 trillion per year preparing for and waging war. However impossible it may seem even to imagine establishing a trillion dollars-per-year fund for any purpose other than world war, such an extraordinary goal has become absolutely necessary in order to inspire any realistic hope at all for sustainability as we approach the twenty-first century.

Life on earth will become sustainable only when enough people stop ignoring the twentieth century warnings of unprecedented danger and begin applying more of their imagination, talent, effort, and money to preparing for and waging peace with even greater determination and sacrificial generosity than we usually devote to wars, floods, earthquakes, hurricanes, tornadoes, and other severe threats.

A cooperative appeal

Thousands of effective organizations are already engaged to the limit of their resources in many of the types of work required to achieve sustainability for life on earth. Most of them appeal regularly to governments, foundations, and concerned citizens for the necessary funds to continue or to expand their work.

Instead of competing expensively with each other in hundreds of individual fund-raising efforts, many organizations will realize far greater success by undertaking a bold, cooperative campaign to fund a total, all-out, global plan for waging peace. No single organization can do it alone, but working together and raising funds together their collective strength will be able to move mountains.

The challenges they face include making a fundamental change in our stewardship of the earth and life on it by initiating an unparalleled revolution in our way of thinking about our future.

A campaign to invest one trillion dollars per year in waging peace

The campaign will invite substantial, even sacrificial, investment in the huge amount of work required to carry out our responsibility for the survival and well-being of the planet and its life for the next seven generations.

Investors will not receive any financial dividends. They will not even recover the capital they invest. They will be investing their money and their effort in anticipation of far more valuable returns: avoiding unparalleled catastrophe and achieving full employment for virtually everyone around the world by actually doing the most satisfying work imaginable—protecting the earth against terracide (killing the earth) and defending life on earth against omnicide (killing everything including *homo sapiens*).

Some people may roll their eyes and shake their heads over such an outrageous goal as $1,000,000,000,000 per year. Proponents of this bold investment campaign will certainly be reminded that we hear every day about gross deficits, government cut-backs in services, and corporate downsizing of personnel, all caused by an allegedly unalterable global state of affairs called TINA—"There Is No Alternative." [2]

In truth, there really are alternatives. There is money in the world. [3] Much more of it will become available to support the most urgently needed work of our troubled global society when concerned groups and individuals cooperate to identify the work priorities of our times, and assemble sufficient financial investments to meet our unprecedented global requirements for sustainability.

Much of the world's wealth belongs to a few very rich people. *The New Internationalist* reported in 1994 that "Between 1987 and 1993 the number of billionaire families and individuals more than doubled, from 98 to 233." One year later, in 1994, 358 billionaires were counted.

> In 1960 the richest one-fifth of the world's people were
> 30 times richer than the poorest fifth. By 1991 they were
> 61 times richer. . . . The world's richest 101 individuals
> and families . . . control wealth valued at some $452
> billion. This is more than the total yearly income of the
> entire population of India, Pakistan, Bangladesh, Nigeria
> and Indonesia put together: one-and-a-half billion
> people in all. . . .[4]

Only 4 of the 101 richest billionaires in the world are women.

Even in the more affluent industrialized countries of the world,
most people are not really rich and some are very poor. Many of us
are deeply concerned about the unconscionable gulf that is growing
even wider now between outrageous wealth and utter poverty.

Thousands of appeal letters go out each year from worthy
organizations desperately requesting donations. If a concerned
family has $300 to contribute, where will it do the most good?
Cancer research? A community development project in Bangladesh?
Amnesty International? Multiple Sclerosis Society of Canada?
Canadian Centre for Policy Alternatives? Oxfam? The David Suzuki
Foundation? A local foodbank? Divide it among several charities?
Or maybe just concentrate it all on one favourite?

What will this family do when an opportunity becomes available
to invest its $300 in a trillion dollars-per-year campaign to provide
substantial funding for hundreds of thousands of programmes
that are bold and creative enough to offer genuine hope for global
sustainability?

With that rewarding possibility in mind, this couple may decide
to invest $3,000 instead of $300. Some people will be able and
willing to invest much, much more in such a high-benefit, non-
profit venture. Others cannot invest any dollars at all without making
an extreme sacrifice. Inspired by this global dream, however, even
low income and unemployed families may devise some way to invest
a few of their scarce dollars or some of their time, energy, and
imagination.

A report released in 1998 by four Canadian departments, including Statistics Canada, showed that lower income families actually contributed a larger percentage to charities than higher income families.

> Although donors with higher incomes tend to make larger donations than do donors with lower incomes, they do not contribute a greater percentage of their pre-tax household income. When one's annual donation is expressed as a percentage of pre-tax household income, donors in lower household income categories gave a larger proportion of their income in financial donations than did those in higher income groups.[5]

Among the reasons given for not donating at all or for not donating more, a few respondents said "it is hard to find a cause worth supporting." An even smaller number agreed that they do not donate, or do not donate more, because "they do not know where to make a contribution."[6]

As for millionaires and billionaires—who knows? If even a few of them become enthused, they will certainly enliven the trillion dollars-per-year campaign.

Responsible wealth

Reliable good news has been so rare in the twentieth century that our first response to any forward-looking proclamation is cautious, at least, if not openly skeptical. In December 1997 a Founding Forum in New York City launched a remarkable new project called Responsible Wealth.[7] It is a major undertaking by United for a Fair Economy, an organization of wealthy people who are deeply concerned about the dangerously expanding division between a dominant, rich minority and the great majority of people who have much less affluence and far less influence.[8] The project has headquarters in Boston and its initial outreach is mainly across the United States.

Is responsible wealth an oxymoron? I think not. By helping to lead the way toward beneficial new modes of thinking, this project appears to offer a genuine ray of hope for the twenty-first century. It may even represent one first small step toward the quantum leap we so desperately need for eliminating yet another long-established wall, after the astonishing collapse in 1989 of the solid Berlin Wall.

Our current, troublesome socio-economic wall is not made of stone and steel, but it just as firmly separates a ruling minority of extremely wealthy people on earth from the rest of us.

This bold new project is clearly explained in its mission statement:

> Responsible Wealth is a group of business people, investors and wealthy individuals among the top 5% of income earners and asset holders in the US (over $125,000 household income and/or $500,000 net assets) who are concerned about growing economic inequality, and are joining together to publicly address the problem. As beneficiaries of economic policies that are tilted in our favor, we feel a responsibility to speak out and change the system to benefit the common good. Our priorities are: 1) educating our members and others about economic inequality and its harmful consequences, and 2) speaking out to our peers, the media, and decisionmakers in support of proposals to close the economic gap.[9]

A call to action

Responsible Wealth describes itself as "a group of people with substantial earned or inherited wealth. As founders, family members or beneficiaries of some of the largest enterprises in America, we have earned or inherited wealth far beyond our needs during our lifetimes."

In their "Call To Action" they explain,

> We feel compelled to speak out, as part of the larger movement for economic justice, about the growing gap between the very rich and everyone else in American society, and against government policies and private corporate practices that are widening this gap.

Concentration of Wealth

In 1976, the wealthiest 1% of the population owned 19% of all private wealth. The top 1% now owns almost 40% of all private wealth, which exceeds the wealth owned by the bottom 92% of the population combined. We believe this increasing concentration of wealth in the hands of the few deprives the many of good wages and the financial resources they need to live comfortably and securely.

Trickle Up

In the 1980s, our nation enacted policies to relieve the tax burden on large corporations and the wealthy on the theory that they would use the additional money in ways that would benefit everyone. It is now generally recognized that this policy did not work. In fact, most income growth in the last 15 years has gone to the top income earners while most lower and middle income households lost ground.

As wealthy people, we personally benefited from the income tax cuts, the cuts in capital gains taxes and the many other policy changes that rewarded large asset-owners. But the majority of Americans did not benefit, and the nation is now saddled with an astronomical national debt and annual budget deficits, due in part to the loss of income from the upper tax brackets. Between 1983 and 1989 alone, the combined assets of the richest 500 families in America increased from $2.5 trillion to $5 trillion; this increase was *three times* the increase in the national debt during that same period.

Lack of Fairness

We believe the rules governing our economy are unfairly tilted in our favor. We recognize that capital and assets play an essential role in building wealth and prosperity in our communities. However, we believe there is an overemphasis on the rights and rewards of private capital. We are faced with a situation where those of us with large amounts of capital are able to pass on fortunes from generation to generation and multiply our wealth through passive investing, while around us, one in four children are born into poverty, and many in our economy have little hope of improving their financial situation.

We believe that in a healthy economy, workers should earn a fair compensation, and all citizens should have the opportunity to earn, save and be economically secure. We believe that civil rights and economic rights are inseparable; we will never have one without the other.

Loss of Community

We believe that the pursuit of the trappings of wealth has overrun the basic understanding of what American society is supposed to be about. We believe that the extent of economic inequality and the scapegoating of society's poorest segments—welfare recipients, immigrants, etc.— are dividing our nation and undermining our collective sense of community.

We believe that the ultimate effect of allowing the canyon between the wealthy and most Americans to continue to grow will be to destroy the basic unifying spirit of a democratic society, something that no amount of material goods can ever replace. By continuing to separate ourselves economically, we are contributing to a society in which people at one end of the economic spectrum are walled off in gated communities while many at the other end of the spectrum are behind bars.

For all of the above reasons, we are speaking out against the policies and practices which narrowly benefit only the most affluent households and undermine the economic security of everyone else.

We call upon elected officials to squarely address the economic divide facing the nation and the rising economic insecurity facing more and more citizens. We ask that they investigate the dangerous consequences of further polarization of income, wages and wealth, and weigh each policy choice with a commitment to closing the divide.

The national debt now exceeds $5 trillion. In the effort to reduce the national debt, we urge that the largest burden of responsibility be placed on the wealthiest Americans, since we benefited the most from the regressive policy changes of the 1980s that fueled the debt.

We call upon elected officials to institute dramatic campaign finance reforms to buffer our democratic process from the undue influence of concentrated wealth, and return the control of our democracy to voters.

We call upon the media to tell the story of the costs and harm to our society of widening inequality, of the damage to our economy, our environment, our democracy, our sense of community, and our spiritual and civil lives.

We call upon other privileged US citizens and business leaders to join us in working for a stronger commonwealth, to strengthen the bonds of our nation and reduce inequality, and to remember that much of our wealth and privilege comes not from our own ingenuity and effort, but from the labor of others, and from the biased rules governing our economy.

We are people who value our privacy and do not wish to be subjected to great media attention. But we feel compelled to speak out because of concern for our fellow citizens and the future of our country. We believe that our best interests incorporate more than just our financial interests, and that our country is capable of doing better.[10]

Some rich people are already investing significantly in sustainability. Two of the twelve members of the initial Organizing Committee for Responsible Wealth are Christopher Mogil and Anne Slepian, authors of an inspiring 1992 book, *We Gave Away a Fortune: Stories of people who have devoted themselves and their wealth to peace, justice and a healthy environment.*[11]

A next step toward waging peace in the twenty-first century will be to spread the astonishing good news of Responsible Wealth beyond the U.S.A. throughout the troubled world of wealth, poverty, and war.

Trustworthy management for the trillion dollars-per-year fund
Who will receive, keep safe, and wisely distribute these dollars?

Before any such cooperative investment campaign is launched, a credible, trustworthy, global institution will have to be established to receive and caretake all these investments. This distinguished board of trustees will distribute financial support wisely to projects which will each be committed to doing its full share of the work required, both regionally and globally. That work must include some promising action for reducing or even eliminating the presently widening chasm between extreme affluence and sickening poverty.

We have now had more than fifty years of experience with such international organizations as the United Nations, the World Bank and the International Monetary Fund (IMF). For example, 1996 was officially designated "The United Nations International Year for the Eradication of Poverty." With only two months left in that year, however, one discouraged observer reminded us all that 1996 was to be the year for *eradicating* poverty, not *exacerbating* it! With greatly increased strength and cooperation among dedicated NGOs, we will be able to avoid familiar pitfalls, and take full advantage of everything we have learned from all the struggles of oppressed and exploited people.

In Chapter 7 I will outline some possible ways to begin identifying or creating, if necessary, a respected body of forward-thinking statesmen, stateswomen, aboriginal elders, scientists and other dedicated persons to whom this great responsibility for a waging peace fund might be entrusted.

Small Is Beautiful and large also has its place

In 1973 E.F. Schumacher wrote in his persuasive book, *Small Is Beautiful,*

> We always need both freedom and order. We need the freedom of lots and lots of small, autonomous units, and, at the same time, the orderliness of large-scale, possibly global, unity and coordination. When it comes to action, we obviously need small units, because action is a highly personal affair, and one cannot be in touch with more than a very limited number of persons at any one time. But when it comes to the world of ideas, to principles or to ethics, to the indivisibility of peace and

also of ecology, we need to recognize the unity of mankind and base our actions upon this recognition.

He emphasized the "*duality* of the human requirement when it comes to the question of size: there is no single answer. For his different purposes man needs many different structures, both small ones and large ones, some exclusive and some comprehensive."[12]

Any campaign to attract investments up to $1 trillion annually will obviously be large. However, that colossal fund will nourish hundreds of thousands of small regional programmes and many global or international projects as well. For example, it could provide $1 million per year to one million NGOs, or $100,000 per year to each of 10 million programmes.

Waging war goes unfettered; Waging Peace needs support

The fall of the Berlin Wall in 1989 ended the Cold War but did not initiate any warm peace. The collapse of Communism did, however, open the way for an unprecedented expansion of capitalism around the world. In his September 1998 article, "Protecting War: Militarism and The Multilateral Agreement on Investment (MAI)," Steven Staples wrote, "Globalization has given rise to huge transnational corporations whose wealth and power now exceed those of nation states, and whose interests transcend national borders." He provides a new label for the old concept of a "military-industrial complex." Because of the enormous increase in corporate power, his modern term is the "military-corporate complex."

The anticipated "peace dividend" never did fulfill its promise to transfer a significant amount of military expense into an effective program to end poverty among the neediest people on earth.

"In fact," Staples reported,

> the end of the Cold War has shifted the entire international paradigm: international diplomacy has been replaced with international marketing; nuclear weapons-free zones with free-trade zones; Third World debt with IMF [International Monetary Fund] bail-outs; and

disarmament summits with the latest free-trade deals.
Even the United Nations itself has been superceded in
influence by the World Trade Organization. . . .

The end of the cold war actually brought us "the amorality of the
free market system which has played itself out in dozens of wars
raging around the world, the globalization of the arms trade, the
reckless expansion of NATO, and the increasing likelihood of
nuclear war."

The Steven Staples essay explains how social programs will be
threatened and military spending protected by the MAI. Restrictions
in the MAI on government-owned enterprises threaten state-run
crown corporations, and could endanger even government-funded
hospitals. MAI prohibitions on "unfair expropriations" will force
governments to compensate foreign corporations for any losses
they claim because of environmental, labour, and human rights
regulations and other legislation they blame for reducing their profits.

"While the MAI threatens nearly every public sector of the
Canadian economy such as health care, education and culture, only
actions or programs implemented in the interest of national security
are explicitly excluded from the liberalizing demands of the MAI,"
says Staples. Specifically, this allows unfettered government spending
for the military, weapons development and production, and direct
support for weapons corporations.

Staples points to the irony that "many OECD [Organization for
Economic Cooperation and Development] countries are trying to
negotiate similar exceptions from the MAI for their health and
cultural sectors—with varying success. But on the issue of military
spending and arms production, the negotiators are in complete
agreement: the military must continue to enjoy government support
without interference."

In Canada, the Department of National Defence maintains an
influential network of contacts within university faculties, research
labs, the media, community associations such as the Canadian
Legion, and corporations which profit from billions of dollars in
military contracts. "Together," Staples declares,

> this paramilitary civil society and the fusion of the
> interests of the military and corporations can be
> understood as the military-corporate complex. . . . The
> corporations are organized into influential lobby groups
> such as the Canadian Defence Industries Association
> and the Aerospace Industries Association of Canada.

The Staples article also provides significant information about
arms exports:

> Like Canada's high military spending, most Canadians
> have no idea that Canadian-made weapons and
> component parts are exported around the world.
> Ironically, while Canadian peacekeepers face warring
> factions around the world Canadian weapons
> corporations are busily exporting more than $1 billion
> in arms each year. . . . a third of Canada's customers are
> in the Third World, making Canada the 8th largest
> exporter of arms to the Third World. In 1996, more
> than $100 million of arms were sold to countries at war
> and a nearly equal amount were sold to a dozen countries
> whose citizens suffer human rights abuses at the hands
> of their own governments.[13]

Back in September 1995 when some U.S. leaders wanted to slash
$1 trillion from spending on the elderly, the sick, the poor, the young,
low paid workers and the environment, David Morris wrote,
"Balance the Budget by Cutting Military Waste." He quoted Charles
Peters, editor of *The Washington Monthly*: "Much of the money wasted
by government is wasted on the military." Republican Senator
Charles Grassley of Iowa was asking, "Why is it that members of
my side of the aisle send their management principles on vacation
whenever the defense budget is mentioned?"

"Military spending today," Morris wrote,

> is higher than in 1980, when Russia invaded Afghanistan
> and the Cold War was in full battle cry. . . . Our military
> budget is nearly as large as the military budgets of all
> the nations of the world combined. It is 17 times more

than the combined military spending of the six countries
the Pentagon sees as our most likely adversaries. . . .
The Pentagon wants the capacity to fight two
simultaneous wars without any allies. Former high
ranking military officers and defense experts across the
ideological spectrum view that objective as absurdly self-
serving and wildly wasteful.

David Morris responds to the advice from Congress telling us
that we have to make hard choices. Both Democrats and
Republicans, he reports,

refuse to allow us to choose to cut military spending
rather than social spending. . . . Fearful that those affected
by proposed budget cuts will rise up and demand military
spending cuts instead, Republicans propose to require a
60 percent Congressional majority before reductions in
military spending can be used to pay for domestic
programs.[14]

This problem is not limited to the United States. When decisions
are made on the use of tax dollars, it seems that abundant military
spending is generally untouchable, even when it is unjustified and
wasteful and threatens the survival of life on earth.

The MAI would protect, promote, and generously fund the
military-corporate complex engaged in waging or preparing for war.
At the same time it would undermine, discourage, and obstruct
funding for waging peace efforts.

I agree with Steven Staples that:

Instead of the MAI, multilateral institutions need to
acknowledge the causes of war, and create international
agreements which not only permit but encourage the
meeting of basic human needs, democracy, and a respect
for human rights. Destructive trade and investment
agreements which do not enhance the vital contribution
of social programs must be replaced with international
agreements which discourage the causes of war and build
institutions needed for peace.[15]

Waging peace will require the combined efforts of NGOs and other concerned citizens to invent alternative funding methods outside of depending on taxes.

A beautiful dream, but what will it take?

Through the twentieth century it has taken an extraordinary amount of bold imagination, courage, money, and sacrifice to fight two World Wars, to overcome some deadly diseases, to unleash the power of the atom, to land on the moon and aim for Mars, to develop automobile and air travel, to produce radio, television and computers, and to achieve many other scientific and sometimes humane miracles.

Now we have come to the end of that century, to the turnaround decade, facing nothing less than the probability of terracide or omnicide unless we very quickly change our modes of thinking and give total, all-out, sacrificial priority to survival.

I am convinced that a fund of $1 trillion per year for Planet Earth and her life is both necessary and possible. What will it take? This whole struggle to provide adequate funding for essential work will certainly benefit from a combination of several motivating attitudes:

- *thoroughly justified, absolute fear*—whether we are rich, poor, or just comfortable—for our own and all future generations of life on earth;
- *confidence* that, since human attitudes and activities are the cause of our global predicament, we human beings can also provide the necessary solutions, by working together—all different colours and cultures, both aboriginal and non-aboriginal—as we give thanks for the help of our Creator;
- *willingness* to dedicate our mental, emotional, economic, social, cultural, artistic, physical, and spiritual gifts to effective cooperative action;
- *appreciation* for the priceless benefits to be gained by all human beings and other life on earth when enough people put a high enough priority on the survival and

well-being of Mother Earth to apply the utmost imagination and cooperative effort to this struggle; and
- *understanding* that unemployment is utterly inexcusable in a world with so much necessary work still to be done and enough wealth on earth to allow those who do this urgently needed (but often non-profit) work to earn a living.

If some of us can dream and do research about building life-supporting conditions on Mars within a century or two,[16] it must be realistic for others of us to invest imagination, money, time, and effort now in keeping our good Earth habitable until Mars is ready for us—or, at the very least, for a few more generations.

. . . keeping our good earth habitable until Mars is ready for us . . .

Notes

1. *Op. cit.*, Chapter 1, Note 29.

2. (a) Ed Finn, "Yes, Virginia (and Virgil), there IS an alternative!" in the *CCPA Monitor*, Ottawa: Canadian Centre for Policy Alternatives, April 1998, p. 4.

    (b) Maude Barlow and Bruce Campbell, *Straight Through the Heart: How the Liberals Abandoned the Just Society*, Toronto: A Phyllis Bruce Book, Harper Collins, 1995.

    In 1991 at a "thinkers' conference" in Aylmer, Quebec, banker Peter Nicholson declared, "What seems beyond question is that the world has entered an era where the objectives of economic efficiency . . . will hold sway virtually everywhere. . . . Societies that fail to respond effectively to the market test can, at best, look forward to a life of genteel decline, and at worst, a descent into social chaos. . . . Today, there is no alternative and, like it or not, the world is in the thrall of global forces that cannot be defied by a relatively small, trade-dependent and massively indebted country like Canada." p. 93.

    In debates on the "excess of democracy" forcing government "to spend beyond its means," the prevailing message was "that there were no alternatives to program cutting: the only question was how much and how fast." p. 133.

    (c) Linda McQuaig, *The Cult of Impotence: Selling the Myth of Powerlessness in the Global Economy*, New York and Toronto: Viking, published by the Penguin Group, 1998.

    "We are told, 'The debt problem has become so extreme that we have no choice but to cut social spending.' This sort of statement is presented as an objective assessment of our situation and often appears in apparently neutral news stories. Now, imagine if a media commentator made the following assertion: 'The debt problem has become so extreme that we have no choice but to raise taxes on the rich.' Such a statement would clearly, and correctly, be seen as the expression of an opinion and would not be acceptable in a neutral news story." pp. 10-11.

3. (a) Ed Finn, "The Money Is There! But governments get less of it," *The Canadian Forum*, January/February 1997, pp. 6,7.

    (b) Howard Pawley, "The money is there, but governments won't collect it," *CCPA Monitor*, Ottawa: Canadian Centre for Policy Alternatives, February 1997.

4. David Ransom, September editor, "Filthy Rich" issue of *The New Internationalist*, Toronto: September 1994, p. 17.

5. Michael Hall, Canadian Centre for Philanthropy: Tamara Knighton, Statistics Canada; Paul Reed, Non-Profit Sector Research Initiative; Patrick Bussiere, Human Resources Development Canada; Don McRae, Canadian Heritage; Paddy Bowen, Volunteer Canada, "Caring Canadians, Involved Canadians: Highlights from the 1997 National Survey of Giving, Volunteering and Participating," Ottawa: Published by authority of the Minister responsible for Statistics Canada, August 1998, p. 8.

6. *Ibid.*, p. 15.

7. Responsible Wealth is a project undertaken by United for a Fair Economy and formally initiated at its Founding Forum in New York City, December 5-6, 1997.

8. United for a Fair Economy is a national organization that draws public attention to the growth of income and wealth inequality in the United States—and to the implications of this inequality for America's democracy, economy and society. Address: 37 Temple Place, 5th Floor, Boston, Massachusetts 02111, telephone (617) 423-2148.

9. "Our Mission," in "Responsible Wealth Update," Vol.2, No.2, Boston: June 1998, p. 2.

10. Responsible Wealth, "A Call to Action," October 1997.

11. Christopher Mogil and Anne Slepian with Peter Woodrow, illustrated by Yani Batteau. *We Gave Away a Fortune: Stories of people who have devoted themselves and their wealth to peace, justice and a healthy environment*, Gabriola Island, B.C. and Philadelphia: New Society Publishers, 1992.

12. E. F. Schumacher, *Small Is Beautiful: Economics as if People Mattered*, New York: Harper Torchbooks, Harper and Row Publishers, 1973, p. 61.

13. Steven Staples, "Protecting war: Militarism and the Multilateral Agreement on Investment (MAI)," a position paper for End the Arms Race, Vancouver: End the Arms Race, September 1998. http://www.peacewire.org/protect.html, pp. 1-16.

14. David Morris, "Balance the Budget by Cutting Military Waste," September 1995. http://www.ilsr.org/columns/26 Sept 95.html.

15. *Op. cit.*, Note 13.

16. (a) Brad Darrach and Steve Petranek, "Can the planet next door be a home away from home by 2170?" or "Can a dead world be brought to life? The Greening of the Red Planet may be the next giant step for mankind," New York: *Life*, May 1991, pp. 24-35.

(b) Sharon Begley, "Next Stop MARS: Twenty-five years after the moon landing, we have the technology to reach the 'red planet.' Do we have the will?," New York: *Newsweek*, July 25, 1994, pp. 42-47.

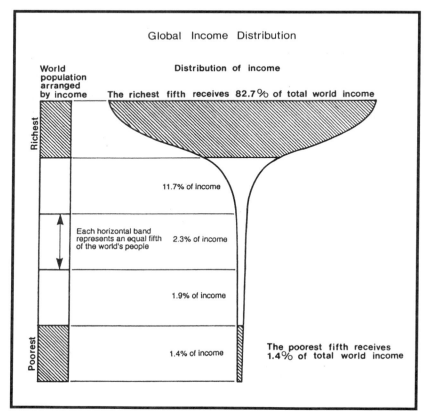

Source: UNDP, *Human Development Report 1992* (New York: Oxford University Press, 1992)

危机 CHAPTER 7

A Plan for One Year
of Waging Peace Research

> Canada has lost the immense amount of output that
> would have been produced by people had they been
> working instead of idle.
> —Economist Ruben Bellan,
> *The Unnecessary Evil*, 1986

Two keys will open the way toward waging peace, with
opportunities for virtually full employment everywhere on earth.
One year of cooperative research will produce these two necessary
keys: a WORK INVENTORY and a FINANCIAL SUPPORT INVENTORY.

Through this book and by other means I am inviting interested
NGOs to put their powerful shoulders behind the development of
WAGING PEACE FOR A LIVING. Anticipating some enthusiastic
responses, in this chapter I propose one scenario for the first year
of a promising action plan.[1]

As I suggested in Chapter 4, some NGOs may wish they could
take part in a waging peace coalition but see no way to spare the
necessary staff, time, or funds to do so. When they respond to my
invitation with an estimate of the additional resources each NGO
requires in order to participate, I am confident that many of us
supporters of the plan will soon find ways to assemble sufficient
funds to overcome any financial obstacle to their involvement.

Initial gathering of a working group of NGO representatives

Whether three or thirty representatives of NGOs get together initially, I presume they will critically review the plan proposed in this book. Whether they adopt or revise that particular action idea or develop a new, superior approach, their discussions will eventually produce an action plan with the added strength of a consensus among some enthusiastic NGOs.

A strong, detailed action plan, likely to earn widespread support, should emerge from this working group before the end of the twentieth century. The working group—the Waging Peace Coalition of NGOs—will also review and revise, if necessary, the approach I am suggesting for beginning the twenty-first century with one year of research to prepare a workable, first draft pair of instruments, the WORK INVENTORY and the FINANCIAL SUPPORT INVENTORY.

Two research teams will prepare the two inventories

One research initiative will produce as comprehensive an inventory as possible in one year of the specific work required to restore long-term health to planet earth and its life.

The other research initiative will produce an inventory of ways to make available sufficient financial and other resources to allow those who actually do this essential work to earn an adequate living.

Some of the appropriate new enterprises will be able to support themselves after getting a start with just a little temporary financial encouragement. However, much of the work that is clearly essential cannot be self-supporting and is not likely to obtain sufficient funding from either government tax sources or from private, corporate philanthropy. In this book I have emphasized the vast amount of important non-profit work that is not being done now, but must be undertaken very soon.

The Work Inventory research plan

Two capable researchers will be selected and employed for one year by some method approved by the working group of the Waging Peace Coalition of NGOs. They will identify what specific work is urgently needed for each of the many relevant fields of work to make its full contribution to sustainable life on earth. There is plenty of work to be done in every country and in a great variety of cultures and circumstances.

These researchers will have sufficient funds in their budget to arrange short-term contracts with as many as 75 advanced but innovative consultants in many fields of work. They will confer with well-informed NGOs not only for specific work proposals, but also for help in selecting appropriate, forward-thinking people to consult about the work required to make substantial, but necessary, changes in each field of work in order to reduce danger and to enhance opportunity for the future.

The WORK INVENTORY research team and its consultants will not have to worry about how to finance all this necessary work. Their creative research will not be limited at all by any question of whether or not the work they are investigating is considered "affordable". Instead, the other crew, the FINANCIAL SUPPORT INVENTORY research team, will be responsible for developing effective ways to pay for whatever work the earth's sustainable future requires.

The Financial Support Inventory research plan

For this research the working group of the Waging Peace Coalition of NGOs will also select or set up a method for selecting two appropriate researchers for the one-year project. These researchers will also have sufficient funds in their budget to arrange short-term contracts with as many as 15 consultants to help them develop a successful, cooperative campaign to raise the unprecedented amount of $1 trillion per year for as many years as it takes to restore health and well-being to the planet and its life.

The team will not only examine all types of available funding resources, but will also invent and perfect alternative methods for cultivating new sources that might not have been available in the past. New possibilities will open up now in view of the broad scope of this research and demonstration project, and considering the urgent need for extensive, innovative work.

Most NGOs are already engaged in work that contributes in some way to the restoring and sustaining objectives of waging peace. By pooling their fund-raising efforts, the participating NGOs will be able to escape from the high cost of their individual, competing campaigns. Furthermore, each one will actually increase its own resources by sharing in the benefits achieved through powerful, cooperative fund-raising.

Many people who donate to NGOs will appreciate a cooperative fund-raising campaign. They may have been receiving scores or even hundreds of requests for donations every year. Many will be willing to contribute more generously to an umbrella fund to help many NGOs strengthen their present work with a significant increase in their resources for the future.

The financial campaign researchers will have in mind the enormous price the world is now paying for military projects, about $1 trillion per year. A comparable amount for waging peace is fully justified.

Four assignments for the year of research

(1) One research team will produce the WORK INVENTORY;

(2) Another will produce the FINANCIAL SUPPORT INVENTORY;

(3) In conjunction with the working group of the NGO coalition, the research staff will also develop a detailed five-year plan (with a budget) for experimental introduction of the inventories in several regional demonstrations where such action has been welcomed. On the strength of these trials, the inventories will be offered for appropriate adaptation to fit the needs of interested communities or countries all around the world.

(4) The research staff will draft for the working group's consideration a plan for trustworthy management of the extraordinary Waging Peace Fund.

Trustworthy management for the fund

A reliable board of trustees will receive, safeguard, and distribute wisely the Waging Peace Fund. All NGOs whose work supports the broad objectives of WAGING PEACE FOR A LIVING will help to choose responsible trustees capable of earning wide respect around the world for their dedication to getting the necessary work underway.

After considering the research team's draft plan for establishing this board of trustees, the working group of the Waging Peace Coalition of NGOs will develop and implement an effective method for securing the services of highly qualified international board members.

Paul LeDuc Browne offered a very useful option in his book, *Love in a Cold World?: The Voluntary Sector in an Age of Cuts*. He suggested:

> the creation of arm's length granting councils to ensure stable core funding for voluntary organizations deemed worthy of grants . . . on the basis of a peer-review type of system. In other words, decisions about allocating grants would not be made by bureaucrats, but by committees made up of people from the voluntary sector itself. Allocations to voluntary organizations could include core funding grants, seed money to start projects, funding for research and the dissemination of its results (publications, special conferences, etc.), and support for sub-sectoral coordinating bodies.[2]

As soon as an internationally respected board of trustees is prepared to endorse it, a cooperative campaign will begin for the Trillion Dollars-Per-Year Fund.

Staffing for the year of research

In addition to the four inventory researchers the project will employ a research coordinator and an office administrator.

The research project coordinator will integrate and coordinate the entire research project including preparing inventories, planning regional demonstrations, and drafting plans for establishing a reliable board of trustees. She or he will ensure that the project completes its four major assignments according to schedule.

When the two inventories are progressing well, all six staff members will begin spending some of their time on the other two assignments. For planning the five-year demonstration project and preparing its budget, the coordinator will work together with the inventory researchers and the office administrator. However, the coordinator will have the primary responsibility for planning all the details for the five-year demonstration project. These will include staff requirements, recruiting, counselling, education/training/ apprenticeship, placement, work spaces, and a demonstration project budget for each of the five years.

When the WORK INVENTORY and the FINANCIAL SUPPORT INVENTORY are completed, the demonstration projects can begin. Each demonstration region can use these two instruments to enable enthusiastic people, including those who are unemployed, to find appropriate work with the help of any counselling, education, training, placement, apprenticeship, or funding services needed.

The coordinator will also carry first responsibility for presenting to the working group of the NGO coalition a draft plan to establish a reliable board of trustees for creating, managing, and distributing the large, long-range waging peace fund.

The office administrator will be responsible for accurate accounting and staying within budget limits; for organizing and maintaining secretarial services; for cooperating with other staff to meet the project's needs for office work, and preparation of effective brochures, reports, and letters; and for negotiating solutions to these and other challenges as they may arise.

All six staff members must be capable of working together effectively. They will all be enthusiastic about the project's ambitious objective: to facilitate necessary changes from prevailing modes of thinking to new ways of living and earning a living appropriate to the requirements for twenty-first century life on earth.

Notes for a research budget

For consideration by the working group of the Waging Peace Coalition of NGOs, I have included as Appendix III a detailed budget for the one year of research. It is only a draft subject to revision, but I want to comment here on some of its features.

Salaries and benefits are provided for one research project coordinator, four researchers (two for each inventory) and one office administrator.

A substantial amount is budgeted to allow the WORK INVENTORY research team to employ, under short-term contracts, one or more forward-thinking consultants in each field of work. The FINANCIAL SUPPORT INVENTORY research team will also have contract funds to employ imaginative consultants to help design an innovative campaign to inspire global investments in waging peace comparable to the world's current expenses for waging war.

Endangered as we are now by our accelerating drift toward unparalleled catastrophe, and challenged at the same time by opportunities for a significantly higher quality of life, we will certainly find the necessary resources for an enthusiastic response.

No doubt the cost of producing the inventories and doing the planning could be reduced if qualified volunteers did part or all of this research project. I suggest, however, that the entire staff and all the consultants should receive full payment for their services. Any researcher or consultant who does not need full pay is welcome to invest as much as possible in the Trillion Dollars-Per-Year Fund.

Notes

1. See Appendix II: A Draft Timetable for Waging Peace, and Appendix III: A Draft Budget for the One-Year Research Project.

2. Paul LeDuc Browne, *Love in a Cold World?: The Voluntary Sector in an Age of Cuts*, Ottawa: Canadian Centre for Policy Alternatives, 1996, p. 57.

危机 CHAPTER 8

The Unaffordable "Unnecessary Evil"

> Everyone has the right to work, to free choice of employment, to just and favourable conditions of work and to protection against unemployment.
> —*Article 23, Universal Declaration of Human Rights*, 1948

Three questions about unemployent are critical to any discussion of the survival and well-being of life on earth, today and for many tomorrows. Is unemployment really necessary? Can we, the people, together with our businesses and our national governments, actually afford the high cost of unemployment? Can planet earth afford the impact of unemployment? This chapter presents compelling evidence that unemployment is not only unaffordable and unhealthy: it is also unnecessary and therefore inexcusable.

Mainstream economic theorists today argue that a certain fairly high level of unemployment is necessary to keep inflation under control. The Business Council on National Issues, the Fraser Institute, the C.D. Howe Institute, the World Bank, the International Monetary Fund, and the Finance Minister of Canada all agree. There may be different views on the precise level of unemployment that must be considered "natural," but when it starts to decline, financial interests begin to worry and demand "corrective" action! Wealthy individuals and transnational corporations who keep a close eye on the stock market will not tolerate "too much" employment.

Professor A.W. Phillips of the London School of Economics examined British statistics for the period 1861 to 1957 and noted a relationship between the unemployment rate and the price level. He suggested that the British price level would likely remain stable only if the unemployment rate stayed as high as about 2.5 per cent.

Economics Professor Ruben Bellan in Winnipeg explained this "Phillips Curve" in a remarkable 1986 book (which should have become a best seller, in my opinion), *The Unnecessary Evil: An Answer to Canada's High Unemployment*. "Subsequent writers," he said,

> elaborated on the relationship that Phillips first discerned. A 'trade-off' was declared to exist between unemployment and inflation: the more there was of one, the less there was bound to be of the other. In every country, it was said, there existed a 'natural rate of unemployment,' and great difficulty would ensue if the actual unemployment rate ever fell below this 'natural' level. A sophisticated version was the NAIRU—non-accelerating inflation rate of unemployment; if ever the actual unemployment rate of a country went below its NAIRU, the country's inflation rate would be bound to go up.[1]

Is there any such thing as a "natural" rate of unemployment? In Bellan's view,

> Unemployment and inflation have not been afflictions of nature like floods, droughts, tornadoes, and volanic eruptions. They have been the consequences of human action. Had people acted differently there would have been much less—conceivably none or virtually none—of both unemployment and inflation.[2]

Economist Bellan disputes the "sophisticated economic doctrine" that "now declares it to be absolutely necessary to have an unemployment rate of at least 7 or 8 per cent—that is, the number of unemployed in Canada must never be less than 1 million." Otherwise the inflation problem will dangerously increase.

With his professional tongue firmly pressed into his cheek, Professor Bellan offers an outrageously "modest proposal":

In effect, unemployed Canadians are to be the country's shock troops in the battle against inflation. It's hardly caricature to suggest that unemployed persons might be given a badge on which is inscribed the proud word 'UNEMPLOYED,' identifying them as members of the gallant army that is protecting the country from inflation.

To maintain that army at the necessary strength, the government is urged to apply sufficiently restrictive economic policies so that at least a million Canadians will always be without jobs. Whether they liked it or not, unemployment would be imposed on them. A believer in freedom of choice would suggest that as an alternative way of recruiting the necessary million-strong army of unemployed, the government might invite people to volunteer, appealing to old-fashioned patriotism or offering some kind of inducement not to work. It could shame them into not working. In England during World War I patriotic ladies standing at intersections handed white feathers to sturdy young men who passed by wearing civilian clothes. If there weren't enough unemployed in Canada, the government could recruit ladies to hand white feathers to persons about to enter their places of work.

Something like this has actually been happening in Canada. Unemployed men and women have staged angry demonstrations, demanding work. The people who demonstrated in this way have been condemned for making unreasonable, intemperate demands. They have been accused of selfishly refusing to recognize that their joblessness is vitally needed to hold down inflation.

The term 'welfare bum' was coined years ago to apply to individuals who lived off public welfare financed by the rest of the community. Unemployed people who today demand jobs could be called 'work bums'; they are demanding employment for themselves that would burden the rest of the community.[3]

The deficit

For many years great myths about "the deficit" have dominated the news, politics, and "expert" opinions by elite economic think tanks. A 1996 booklet by Duncan Cameron and Ed Finn exposed these myths. It was published by the Canadian Centre for Policy Alternatives: *Ten Deficit Myths: The truth about government debts and why they don't justify cutbacks.* Myth Number 6 promotes the mistaken notion that "The deficit causes recessions, high interest rates, and high unemployment." In fact, the authors explain,

> Blaming our worst economic ills on the deficit is standing truth on its head. **The truth is the exact opposite: the deficit is caused by recessions, high unemployment and high interest rates.** . . . *the deficit is no more the cause of our economic illness than sneezing and coughing are the cause of colds.*[4]

In a persuasive analysis of Canadian statistics, Bellan suggests "Fewer Jobs, Higher Deficits." In four succinct paragraphs he encourages us to think about lowering the deficit by reducing unemployment:

> In the 49 years since 1946, Canada's unemployment rate was under 5% in 17 years, over 7% in 22 years, and between 5% and 7% in nine years.
>
> In every year that the unemployment rate was under 5%, the federal government had a budget surplus. In every year that the unemployment rate was over 7%, it had a deficit. In the nine years in which the unemployment rate was between 5% and 7%, it had five deficits and four surpluses.
>
> These figures should surprise no one. Unemployed Canadians don't contribute tax revenue to the government; instead they draw on it through unemployment insurance and welfare, and generate social problems that require additional government outlays.
>
> Judging by the factual record, an economic strategy designed to end Ottawa's deficit will succeed only if it sufficiently lowers the country's unemployment rate. There is no possibility of a balanced federal budget so long as the national unemployment rate remains at 9 to 10%.[5]

The global economy

Global Dreams by Richard J. Barnet and John Cavanagh must be the most exhaustive and thoroughly documented report ever written on the new world economy which is now completely dominated by a few transnational corporations, elite economic think-tanks, and wealthy families, with very little left of the former democratic control by powerful, sovereign nations. "Over the past two decades," the authors wrote in 1994,

> images of consumption have been transmitted across the planet, but for most of the world the dreams are unrealizable for both economic and psychological reasons. About two-thirds of the people on earth cannot connect most of the glamorous products they see on billboards and on television with their own lives of poverty and struggle. The expanding cornucopia of globally distributed goods is largely irrelevant to the basic needs of most people in the world.[6]

Take shoes, for example:

> In 1980 the wholesale market for athletic shoes of all sorts in the United States was $7.6 billion . . . This extraordinary popularity of fancy sports footwear is largely due to the aura surrounding these products from endorsements by Michael Jordan and other global sports figures. For promoting Nikes across the globe Jordan reportedly received $20 million in 1992, an amount greater than the entire payroll of the Indonesian factories that make them.[7]

The prevailing market system operates, of course, on "supply and demand." In the past couple of decades, however, computer-operated robots and a globalized "free" economy have made it increasingly possible for industry and private contractors to supply nearly all the goods and services demanded, with only a minimum of paid workers. In fact, productivity continues to escalate even while corporations and governments drastically "downsize" the number of their employees.

As Angus Reid reported in *Shakedown*, "So efficient has the world become that many people are no longer needed even as consumers. By 1995 almost one-third of the world's 2.8 billion workers were either unemployed or clearly underemployed." [8]

Reid reminds us that

> the horse is passé, replaced by the steam locomotive, the tractor and the automobile. Once horses had outlived their usefulness to humans, they started to disappear. . . There's an eerie similarity between the irrelevance of horses to twentieth century economies and the growing irrelevance of large numbers of human beings to the labour forces of the twenty-first.[9]

Poor people, whether they are low income workers or unemployed, cannot participate in either supply or demand because they are excluded from the productive economy and have no way to pay for anything.

Globalization as a deliberate scheme

Dr. Vandana Shiva is a distinguished and outspoken global economist in India. Her conception of globalization will surprise some people who depend heavily on established media, elite economic think-tanks, and their political leaders to explain this phenomenon. An overwhelming flood of propaganda keeps telling the world that globalization is just happening. You can't stop it. It is natural and it is inevitable. Furthermore, they say, it will increase prosperity for everyone.

At the opening of a four-day seminar in 1998, speaking at Simon Fraser University on "Women, Life and the Planet," [10] Vandana Shiva made it clear that globalization is not just "happening." "Globalization," she declared, "is the ultimate project of capitalist patriarchy. Projects don't just happen; they are designed to happen; they are intended; they are shaped. Very often they are shaped through coercion and silencing."

The phenomenon we call globalization is a project that has taken half a century to develop. It is misrepresented to us as natural and inevitable, but it has actually been designed by certain people and it represents their values. It did not emerge out of any general consensus or intercultural dialogue. It is not based on a concern for all beings or even for all people. Its theme is "Let me grab as much as I can right now."

Money may beget more money, but the real creators of genuine wealth are nature and people, not capital. Globalization, which was supposed to increase prosperity for all, has now almost completely detached wealth from any real economy. U.S. $4 trillion of capital are flitting about the world daily. Now money has acquired a life of its own. Dr. Shiva calls it "hungry wealth." This money needs to invest itself in order to make money out of money.

This fictitious money is based on speculation, on money trading. A quarter century ago most money reflected access to real goods and services. Today, 97.5 percent of money is speculative, created out of people playing a game, betting on it, casino style.

The onset of a speculative economy has reduced the real economy to a tiny amount. Now only 2.5 percent of money is involved with real goods and services.

"As we all know," Vandana Shiva said, " patriarchal politics has always been called natural. Women are the second sex. That is nature. Coloured people are second class, to be put down. That is nature. Globalization is just natural."

Natural? Inevitable? There is nothing natural or inevitable about what is going on. Globalization is purposefully structured into all our free trade agreements which deny the need to regulate inequality. Now the corporation has acquired protection and legal rights as a person while the white men who run it escape responsibility through their status as individuals.

The architects of globalization assured the world that the wealth it creates would feed a huge increase in investments and jobs. This well advertised "trickle-down" feature never did materialize. Instead, high unemployment continues under globalization and the gap between rich and poor grows ever wider.

The high cost of unemployment

What does unemployment actually cost? The human costs of unemployment have multiplied during the past decade, even in wealthy countries like Canada, because government and corporate downsizing has pushed so many more people into either the agonies of unemployment or the constant fear of it.

In his comments on "restrictive fiscal and monetary policies" Ruben Bellan wrote,

> But while they may be successful against inflation and easy to apply, policies that impose large-scale unemployment involve enormous cost. They cause economic waste . . . lost output and human trauma in the form of frustration and bitterness, both on an immense scale. And they typically impose the burden of sacrifice primarily upon the community's weakest members—those who have the least market power and are the first victims of overall economic contractions.[11]

In a 1983 report for the Canadian Mental Health Association, *Unemployment: Its Impact on Body and Soul*, Sharon Kirsh wrote:

> In our country of relative wealth, over two million adults want jobs and cannot find them.
> The federal government estimates that it will pay $12 billion in 1983 in the form of jobless benefits (*Toronto Star*, April 30, 1983). If we calculate unemployment insurance payments, welfare costs, foregone income, profits, and taxes, then the cost to Canada of this year's unemployment will be in the order of $50 billion (Social Planning Council of Metropolitan Toronto in the *Globe and Mail*, May 3, 1983).[12]

How could these costs be so enormous? It is partly because the actual amount of unemployment is much more than government reports reveal. The Kirsh report was based on 1982 data but, nevertheless, her "Summary Fact Sheet" is still valid. She makes it clear that "most official statistics underestimate reality." Consider her 1982 facts:

- Canada's real level of unemployment is over 2 million people
- Canada's real unemployment rate is over 19 percent
- the 1982 unemployment rate was the highest recorded since 1938-39 [Great Depression years just prior to World War II]
- youth (ages 15-24 years) have the highest rates of unemployment
- the unemployment rate among female heads of households (lone employed mothers) is 65 percent greater than for male heads of households.

Official unemployment statistics always need correction upward. It is necessary to add those workers who want and desperately need full-time meaningful employment, but can only find part-time work that does not fully use their abilities or challenge their interests. Also add those who have become discouraged by so many rejections that they have stopped looking for work and no longer count in official statistics.

It is often repeated in economics and in politics these days that we have to tolerate a bit of short-term pain in order to achieve significant long-term gain. Most of the pain, however, falls on the backs of people who are not rich, especially those who are unemployed or otherwise poor. Their pain includes malnutrition and even starvation for too many people around the world, together with an absence of hope that they may find some way to earn an adequate family income.

If there is any long-term gain at all from high unemployment, that gain does not include any genuine progress toward restoring health to our planet.

The health cost of unemployment and poverty

Speaking on "Determinants of Health"[13] in 1993, Dr. John Millar, British Columbia's provincial health officer, presented an overview of all the factors that are known to impact on health including some very rough estimates of the contribution made to health by the following factors:

- illness care (less accurately called health care)   25%
- genetics (biological endowment)   15%
- physical environment (clean air, water, food,
  waste disposal, etc.)   10%
- social and economic factors   50%

Social and economic factors contributing to illness include poverty, unemployment, limited education, income maldistribution, lack of social supports, and social injustice.

To elaborate on the factors which make up 50 percent of the determinants of health, I have selected a few quotations from the 77-page *Report on the Health of Canadians.* Prepared in 1996 by the Federal, Provincial and Territorial Advisory Committee on Population Health, it states:

> The rich are healthier than the middle class, who are in turn healthier than the poor. The well-educated are healthier than the less-educated, and the employed are healthier than the unemployed.
>
> Income, education, and employment are all indicators of living and working conditions. These factors affect health by themselves, but also interact with each other. The combined factors of chronic unemployment, inadequate education, inadequate nutrition, and poor housing all contribute to the generally poorer level of health experienced by many Aboriginal communities and by both working and unemployed poor throughout Canada. . . .[14]
>
> Many studies demonstrate that the more equitable the distribution of wealth, the healthier the population. In other words, while the total amount of money in a society is important, it is more important that available income be shared among the population. . . .[15]

Good jobs are related to better health, by providing people with the incomes they need to purchase housing, food, and other necessities. In addition, people who have meaningful work have more choices and control in their lives, and they tend to have better health. The biological explanation for how this could happen is becoming clearer. Recent studies show that limited options and poor coping skills increase vulnerability to a range of diseases, through pathways that involve the immune and hormonal systems. . . .

There is a particular need to address the problem of families living in poverty, particularly those headed by single women. . . .

20% of all children—and 60% of children in female, lone-parent families—live in poverty, and these rates have not been improving. [This is for Canada, even though Canada is a wealthy country.] . . . Children in these circumstances are not able to take full advantage of educational opportunities and are much more likely to have poor health throughout life. Perhaps of greatest concern, children in poverty are unlikely to be able to provide any better conditions for their own children and grandchildren, and so the cycle of disadvantage is passed on from one generation to the next. . . .

Safe workplaces contribute to health. . . .Workplaces can also be made sensitive to the needs of families, through parental leave policies, flexible work arrangements, and the availability of worksite child care.

People who have more control over their work circumstances are healthier. Hence, organizational policies that promote employee participation in corporate decision-making are health-promoting. Health is also affected by stress-related demands of the job, such as the pace of work, the frequency and flexibility of deadlines, and the perceived meaningfulness of the work.

Education acts as a strong influence on health, from the very earliest years of life. . . . education is important not only through the years of formal schooling, but throughout life. It increases opportunities for employment, income security, and job satisfaction. And, education improves people's ability to access and understand information and to make choices that keep them healthy. . . .

Friendship networks in the home, at work, and in community organizations can help us to feel that we have a place in the world, and that we are important in the lives of others. . . .The caring and respect that occurs in social relationships, and the resulting sense of satisfaction and well-being, seem to act as a buffer against health problems. . . .

Housing is important to health in several ways. . . housing that is safe, warm, and dry is a necessity of life. . . . also a home, a place where people can feel secure, a place to keep things that are important to them, and a place to develop a sense of identity and belonging—all factors that can enhance health. . . . When the search for suitable and affordable housing causes people to move frequently, the associated stresses and disruptions of social networks may lead to poorer health. . . .[16]

Suitable, affordable housing is painfully difficult to find for unemployed and underemployed people.

The human cost of unemployment

The human cost of unemployment cannot be adequately measured in dollars. It amounts to nothing less than the cost of despair. Ruben Bellan put it this way:

Worse than the economic loss caused by unemployment is the psychological damage—the shock experienced by people who are laid off and compelled to lower their standard of living, the frustration and bitterness felt by people who spend their days in forced idleness. Heads of families suffer the shame of being unable to provide for their dependants. Studies in the U.S. and the U.K. indicate that higher rates of unemployment bring increases in crime, mental and physical illness, marital breakdown, and suicide. . . .

In respect to Canada, he wrote,

> Certainly the crime rate has increased. Canada's penitentiary population has soared to record levels in the 1980s. Our prisons have become crowded as never before, making it nearly impossible to carry out classification and sorting procedures, to operate programs of counselling and training that aim at rehabilitation. Harassed officials declare that they desperately need the additional prisons that have been projected, but whose construction has been deferred in accordance with the program of economic restraint. 'Double-bunking'—placing two prisoners in a cell designed for one—has been resorted to, with explosive consequences in the form of prison riots.
>
> Economic recession and penitentiary boom are not unrelated. A good many of the individuals who stage burglaries and hold-ups do so because they cannot get work. Persons who leave home in the hope of finding jobs elsewhere have those hopes dashed as regions that have been expanding stagnate instead; some, stranded and penniless, commit crimes to get the money they need to make their way back home.[17]

In her report for the Canadian Mental Health Association, Sharon Kirsh provides a long list of "side effects" of unemployment:

> Copious evidence points to its catastrophic impact on our mental and physical health. For example, we know that with increases in rates of unemployment there are increases in the rates of:
> - depression
> - anxiety
> - self-deprecation
> - fatalism
> - anger
> - spouse abuse
> - child abuse
> - suicide
> - mental hospital admissions
> - homicides and rape

- property crimes
- youth alienation
- children's problems in school
- divorce
- alcoholism
- poverty-induced consequences (e.g. poor nutrition, inadequate housing, etc.)
- fatigue
- weight loss or obesity
- ulcers
- fainting spells
- hard drug abuse
- tobacco abuse
- caffeine abuse
- insomnia
- rapid breathing
- muscle tension
- infant mortality
- heart disease

What are the human issues? There are many and they are complex.

First, paid work is essential for physical survival. . . . Second, paid work is essential for psychological survival. . . .Third, those several segments of society who have traditionally been disenfranchised and denied jobs are finding themselves in increasingly powerless positions as unemployment skyrockets. For example, those who are 'psychiatrically disabled', who have always been in the back wards economically, now find it almost impossible to compete in a job market that looks for workers who are psychologically and physically (relatively) 'flawless'. Any person who is 'flawed' by virtue of her/his physical disability, race, religion, sex, age, sexual orientation, or political orientation is bound to flounder in the labour market—the cards are stacked against those who do not measure up.

A fourth value issue is one of social cost. If unemployment costs Canadian society $50-75 billion in one year, then does it make sense to allow, through social and economic policy decisions, the escalation of job loss? Our society, as an ecological system, suffers when millions of adults are thrown out of work. . . .

> We cannot continue to blame the jobless for their joblessness; we cannot continue to accept the notion that unemployment is a necessary evil, and we cannot continue to develop strategies that barely scratch the surface of an issue so deep and dangerous that it must be plumbed. . . .
>
> The issue of unemployment is global, national, regional, local, and personal. It will require changes by all sectors, and it will require the questioning of our work ethic, our leisure ethic, our power vis-a-vis technological innovations, our power vis-a-vis one another, and our valuation of human life and dignity. . . .We are not powerless to act.[18]

In Ruben Bellan's economics the high human cost of unemployment makes no sense and it ranks first among the unnecessary expenses to be eliminated.

> The waste of unproduced output is not the greatest harm caused by unemployment. Most people who are unemployed suffer frustration from the denial of opportunity to fulfil themselves through work. They live in a succession of formless days that lack the pattern of regular employment; they have only the limited purchasing power of savings, insurance, or welfare.
>
> *No economy, no matter how much it produces, can be considered to be operating acceptably, to be 'recovered' or 'prosperous,' if one worker in ten suffers the trauma of unemployment.* [My emphasis] And the psychological damage extends beyond those who are jobless. A high rate of unemployment causes apprehension among people who still have jobs. Their lives are darkened by the fear that they might also become unemployed. They don't buy things they would like to have for fear they might lose their jobs and would then badly need the money they had spent. They don't quit a job they dislike out of fear that they might not get another one.[19]

The most devastating cost of unemployment is the wasted potential and frustration of hundreds of millions of people around the world, people who want to work but have idleness imposed on them.

The high cost of our proclaimed "healthy economy"

How much does it cost our society when we follow the lead of those influential mainstream economic experts who give our economy a clean bill of health even while unnecessary unemployment remains intolerably costly? I turn once more to Ruben Bellan:

> Much of today's economic reporting and forecasting is in Newspeak. Commentators glowingly declared in 1984 that the Canadian economy had recovered from the 1981-82 recession, although the unemployment rate was still in the double digits, not too far below the levels of the 1930s when Canada experienced the worst depression in history. What's more, the persistence of such rates of unemployment in the future will apparently not prevent Canada from being regarded as prosperous.
>
> The authors of this judgment employ only a single criterion in their assessment of national economic performance: how much is produced. If national output increases by 2 per cent a year, the country is declared to be prosperous, no matter how high the unemployment rate, no matter how unequally the national income is being distributed.
>
> But in any sane assessment of national economic performance, the unemployment rate would be the primary and governing consideration. A low unemployment rate would indicate good economic performance, in that the country was effectively using its potential. A high unemployment rate would unambiguously denote inferior performance: the country would be suffering waste in the form of failure to produce worthwhile goods for which it had the capacity.[20]

The unaffordable expense of unparalleled catastrophe

Who benefits from high unemployment? It may seem attractive to some corporations if they want a crowd of hungry applicants at the gate competing for very few jobs—begging for any kind of work under any conditions, even with minimal pay, high risks, no benefits, or even part time work with no promising future at all.

High unemployment can only please those individuals who are already financially comfortable and care more about maximizing their personal income than about the well-being of other people or their own country or making it possible, somehow, to start doing all the challenging work that is desperately needed to sustain healthy life on earth.

That is the most unbearable expense of high unemployment for our own world: the tragic cost of leaving undone a vast amount of essential work while so many millions of people suffer the agonies of exclusion from opportunities to earn a living by actually doing that work. At a time when so much challenging work is needed to change our modes of thinking and to stop our continuing drift toward unparalleled catastrophe, the cost of unemployment goes beyond any dollar figure. It includes the full price of massive hopelessness.

Mahatma Gandhi's worldview would serve us well in this era of the widening chasm between rich and poor: the earth can provide enough to meet everyone's need but not to satisfy anyone's greed.

During the past quarter century and into the 1990s—that critical "Turnaround Decade" [21]—national governments like ours in Canada have certainly turned around! We have been manipulated into reverse gear. We are moving backward, turned completely away from any forward progress toward universal medical care, fair taxation and reasonably equitable distribution of income and wealth, education for everyone, meaningful employment opportunities for youth and all other people, respect for human rights, and shared responsibility for protecting the planet and life on earth for our own and future generations.

Nowhere on this endangered planet can we afford to allow unemployment—this expensive, unhealthy, and unnecessary evil—to disrupt our global struggle for survival.

Notes

1. Ruben Bellan, *The Unnecessary Evil: An Answer to Canada's High Unemployment*, Toronto: McClelland and Stewart, 1986, p. 24.

2. *Ibid.*, p. 19.

3. *Ibid.*, pp. 146, 147.

4. Duncan Cameron and Ed Finn, *Ten Deficit Myths: The truth about government debts and why they don't justify cutbacks*, Ottawa: Canadian Centre for Policy Alternatives, January, 1996, pp. 18-19.

5. Ruben Bellan, "Fewer Jobs, Fewer Deficits," in *CCPA Monitor*, Ottawa: Canadian Centre for Policy Alternatives, May, 1995, p. 2.

6. Richard J. Barnet and John Cavanagh, *Global Dreams: Imperial Corporations and the New World Order*, New York: A Touchstone Book published by Simon and Schuster, 1994, p. 183.

7. *Ibid.*, p. 328.

8. Angus Reid, *Shakedown: How the new economy is changing our lives*, Toronto: Black Sturgeon Enterprises, published in Canada by Doubleday Canada, 1996, p. 105.

9. *Ibid.*, pp. 127, 128.

10. Vandana Shiva, notes taken by Walt Taylor from a video of a series of talks at the Summer Institute for Women's Studies, June 16 to 19, 1998, "Women, Life and the Planet," at Simon Fraser University, Burnaby, British Columbia. These notes are based on Dr. Shiva's Day 1: "Globalization: the Ultimate Project of Capitalist Patriarchy."

    Dr. Shiva's work is literally about the future of the planet, the future of humanity, the future of all life. She is concerned about the devastation taking place in women's lives as a result of free trade.

11. *Op. cit.*, Note 1, p. 169.

12. Sharon Kirsh, *Unemployment: Its Impact on Body and Soul*, a report prepared for CMHA's National Working Sub-Committee on the Human Impact of Unemployment, Ottawa: Canadian Mental Health Association, 1983, p. v.

13. Dr. John Millar, Provincial Health Minister for British Columbia, "Determinants of Health," Speaking Notes, Summer 1993, pp. 5, 6.

14. The Federal, Provincial and Territorial Advisory Committee on Population Health, *Report on the Health of Canadians* prepared for the Meeting of Ministers of Health in Toronto, September 10-11, 1996, Ottawa: Health Canada Communications and Consultation Directorate, 1996, p. iii.

15. *Ibid.*, p. 48.

16. *Ibid.*, p. 70-73.

17. *Op. cit.*, Note 1, p. 64.

18. *Op. cit.*, Note 12, pp. 98, 99.

19. *Op. cit.*, Note 1, pp. 151, 152.

20. *Op. cit.*, Note 1, p. 151

21. Lester R. Brown, Christopher Flavin, and Sandra Postel, "A Turnaround Decade" in Chapter 10, "Outlining a Global Action Plan," in Worldwatch Institute, *State of the World 1989*, New York: W.W. Norton, 1989, pp. 192-194.

Ben Wicks

危机 CHAPTER 9

Entrepreneurship
and Other Employment Ideas

If you want peace, prepare for peace.
—motto on a wall at the
University for Peace in
Costa Rica

A quarter century ago California was vibrating with changing worldviews, individual and group therapies, and many other exciting new ideas. Carl Rogers was there trying out many applications of his "client-centred," or "non-directive" psychotherapy in a variety of new ways. Among the enthusiastic participants in this mind-boggling deluge of California experiments, both Carl Rogers and Richard Farson were mentioned prominently in a 1966 article in *Look* magazine about "the turned-on people." At one point in his busy, innovative life Dr. Farson took a deep breath and confessed, "I sometimes get the feeling that if one more person comes in here with another great idea, I'll throw him out."[1]

Entrepreneurship
Entrepreneurship has become a widespread buzz word, perhaps the predominant employment notion of the pre-millennial decade. From the French *entreprendre*, to undertake, an entrepreneur is defined as "one who organizes, manages, and assumes the risks of a business or enterprise." One might say that an entrepreneur is an "undertaker", a person who undertakes something that may be risky

but offers potential rewards.

However, a narrow sense of entrepreneurship seems to prevail in these days of downsizing both government and corporate employment. Now is the time, we are told, to emphasize competition over cooperation, self employment over collective enterprise, getting ahead over pulling together, maximizing private profit over protecting the earth. The mutual fund supplants the Canada Pension Plan.

My old French dictionary further enriches the definition of *entreprendre*: "to undertake, to attempt, to take in hand, to take upon one's self; to contract for, to contract to; to adventure, to offer, to venture; to trouble." In that broad sense, any individuals, groups, or coalitions who undertake to wage peace for a living must certainly either be or become entrepreneurs.

In his 1996 book, *Shakedown: How the New Economy is Changing our Lives*, pollster Angus Reid wrote,

> . . . it's time to face the ultimate truth about jobs in the new economy: we're going to have to generate them ourselves. There are two paths along which this will occur, and both begin at the same point: entrepreneurship. This is, of course, one of the decade's sexier words. Many people assume it means a desire to get rich in a climate of unrestrained capitalism. But nothing could be further from the truth. Entrepreneurship is about taking responsibility and creating bold new initiatives,. . . [and]refusal to listen to naysayers standing on the sidelines shouting, 'it can't be done'.
>
> Entrepreneurship isn't about personal greed but it is about ambitious ideas tackled with others in a spirit of cooperation and sharing. Finally, and perhaps most important, entrepreneurs, like human cannon balls, perform best when there's a net.[2]

Without being greedy, an entrepreneur does need to have, borrow, or otherwise obtain enough money to create and implement any good dream plan. Furthermore, that plan must provide enough profit to enable the entrepreneur to earn a living. Angus Reid continued:

> You can't pursue an entrepreneurial dream without money and nobody but the very rich can bring a viable enterprise to fruition without access to credit. Yes, one-person companies are beginning to proliferate, often operated out of the home. And many of these can be bankrolled out of savings, or out of buy-out packages from a company or government. But, by definition, one-person companies create only one job. Canada needs thousands of new companies that each create at least a handful of jobs and, with determination and any kind of luck, more. . . .
>
> My bank manager told me that tight money was good for small business because it forced budding entrepreneurs like me to run profitable operations—or die. His last name was Coffin. . . . A lot of entrepreneurs with good ideas—but no money to invest—will not be starting ventures any time soon.[3]

Much of the great work required for the survival of Earth and essential to the well-being of life on Earth is actually non-profit work. How can dedicated, well-trained, imaginative entrepreneurs even consider tackling any of this work which must be done, but cannot turn a profit? The main purpose of WAGING PEACE FOR A LIVING is to develop feasible answers to that question.

Canadians for Constitutional Money (C.C.M.)

Although the necessary legal and economic information about C.C.M. has not received adequate notice in the established media, compelling evidence is available to support the position that the Bank of Canada could and should provide low-interest loans to public bodies including municipalities, provincial governments, and the federal government. Even at this late date such loans could virtually eliminate the debt and deficit burden which has caused so much unnecessary slashing of health, education, welfare, employment insurance, and other important services, and prompted the denial of urgently needed capital funds to repair or replace deteriorating hospitals, schools, and other vital infrastructure. *The Networker*, a C.C.M. publication, reports "A Creative Solution to Debt and Taxes." The objective of C.C.M., it says,

> is to secure municipal support for an advisory petition calling upon Parliament to instruct the Bank of Canada to issue interest-free loans to tax-supported bodies such as municipalities, hospital and school boards. The use of such loans would be limited to the financing of capital projects which have been voter-approved via single-issue Referenda, and/or for the paying down of present interest-bearing loans negotiated via the Municipal Finance Authority (the M.F.A.), a private consortium of bankers who have established a total monopoly on municipal borrowing. . . .
> . . .international interest and support continue to grow, despite a mass media black-out! *The 300-year tide of usury-driven debt is beginning to turn!*[4]

In Canada, at least, the proper use of the Bank of Canada could eliminate most of the enormous burden of compound interest payments by federal, provincial, and municipal governments. This alone could reduce if not wipe out the deficit hysteria which has been used to force people to accept corporate rule as though it were inevitable and unavoidable.

Shorten the work week

One widely promoted idea for people who have jobs is simply to reduce their working time to 35 or even 32 hours per week. Enthusiasts suggest that the hours of work that would be saved in this way could be shared with people who would otherwise be unemployed. Bruce O'Hara has written extensively about this idea, including "A Detailed Plan for Implementing a Four-Day Workweek in Canada" in *Working Harder Isn't Working; how we can save the environment, the economy and our sanity by working less and enjoying life more.*[5]

In a 1995 article he argued "The case for working less." "Without a reduction in the standard work week, preferably to 32 hours," he predicted, "we can expect to reach an official unemployment rate of 12% after the next recession, and it could go as high as 16%." [6]

O'Hara is dedicated and he means well, but I must disagree. I am surprised to find that many analysts who deplore the current high levels of unemployment finally fall back on the shorter work week as a solution.

In the first place, I do not think a shorter work week would even make a dent in the inexcusably high levels of unemployment and underemployment. As I have shown in Chapter 8, continuing high unemployment does not just happen; it is intentionally designed, a product of corporate will.

Second, O'Hara's idea leaves completely unanswered the challenging problem of too much absolutely essential work that is not getting done simply because it cannot turn a profit.

For some people, when reduced work fits their interests, needs and family circumstances, a shorter work week may be just what the doctor ordered. As a general policy for our whole society, however, the 32-hour week would be a lethal prescription. Jobs may be scarce, but work that needs to be done is not. To respond effectively to our present global and national problems requires so much urgently-needed work that it would keep everyone on Earth fully occupied on a full-time basis for the foreseeable future.

Too many existing jobs are part-time, short-term, poorly paid with no benefits and no future. Millions of underemployed working people want their hours increased, not reduced. Good work does not often come in convenient hourly chunks which can be simply redistributed from those who have too much to those who have little or no paid work. With a 32-hour week many low income workers will eagerly look for a second job to ease their heavy financial pressures. How could that benefit unemployed and underemployed workers?[7]

Job cremation

In our current globalized economy, downsizing prevails in both public services and private enterprises. Governments try to fight debt and deficit problems by slashing funds for public services. While political leaders all advocate "job creation," their persistent budget cuts undermine the quality and availability of important public services, including employment, health, education, welfare, human rights, and environmental restoration and protection, as well as innovative research and development. Reducing waste is one thing, but when governments cut below the waste, that surgery is devastating to public health and well-being. As nurses have warned us all, "Some cuts don't heal!" When governments chop great holes in society's social safety net, that unjustified reduction in services and employment must be denounced as *job cremation*.

In the private sector, downsizing employment offers one way to reduce costs and increase profits. With the rapid development of technology in recent decades, including computers and robotics, it has become possible to increase production and profits while reducing the number of employees. Much of the productive work of the world can now be done with fewer and fewer human workers.

Extrapolated into the twenty-first century, this raises alarming questions: How many of us are really no longer needed? Will many people on earth soon become obsolete?

Downsized corporations with more technology and fewer employees may very well be able to supply the whole world's demand. What they will not provide is any way to reduce the widening chasm between the minority who have the means to be part of the world's demand and the majority who are too poor and/or oppressed to participate in either supply or demand.

"Job creation" is promoted by government as a sort of treatment for the unemployment consequences of massive downsizing. It can be suspect for three reasons. First, too many of the jobs eliminated by downsizing were really valuable and should never have been cut.

Second, job creation sounds to me very much like "make work." In order to "create" any jobs, it seems necessary to "think up" or to "make up" some item to produce or some service to offer and then find a way to sell it. It is shameful when unnecessary and unsatisfying jobs are created mainly to make the unemployment statistics look a little better or to keep unemployed people quiet.

Third, why should we want to "create" any jobs when there is so much work right in front of our noses that urgently needs to be done?

The main question we seem to be asking when we try to create a job is: will it turn a profit after expenses are paid? We need to ask instead: will it benefit our struggle for a sustainable future, or will it actually do harm to society, even while making a financial profit for some people?

Instead of emphasizing only profitable "job creation," we could—and must—begin opening the way for actually doing urgently needed work, even when it cannot pay its own way. We must identify the enormous amount of highly beneficial work that must be done, and at the same time invent effective ways to provide financial support for all that essential work.

"MAI-DAY!"

Secret negotiations underway in Paris may become at least as dangerous to our planet and its life as all the environmental threats described in the *World Scientists' Warning to Humanity*. The early information about the Multilateral Agreement on Investment leaked out in the spring of 1997 and it was first published in *The Nation*.[8]

"MAI-DAY! The Corporate Rule Treaty" by Tony Clarke was published by the Canadian Centre for Policy Alternatives. It provides "A Preliminary Analysis of the Multilateral Agreement on Investments (MAI) which seeks to consolidate global corporate rule." A few paragraphs from Clarke's 12-page analysis will reveal the outrageous arrogance of this secret, elite scheme being planned for corporations to dominate the world.

> Initially, the European Commission (EC) had proposed
> that a global investment treaty be developed as the

centrepiece of the new World Trade Organization (WTO). But the U.S. feared that opposition from developing countries in the WTO would 'water down' any consensus that might be reached on an investment treaty.

The U.S. therefore decided that the best way to achieve a 'high standard' investment treaty was to negotiate it through the rich nations' club of the OECD [Organization for Economic Cooperation and Development]. As U.S. officials have stated, their prime objective is 'to obtain a high-standard multilateral investment agreement that will protect U.S. investors abroad.' To that end, the **MAI is designed to establish a whole new set of global rules for investment that will grant transnational corporations the unrestricted 'right' and 'freedom' to buy, sell, and move their operations whenever and wherever they want around the world, unfettered by government intervention or regulation.**

In short, the MAI seeks to empower transnational corporations through a set of global investment rules designed to impose tight restrictions on what national governments can and cannot do in regulating their economies. The ability of governments, for example, to use investment policy as a tool to promote social, economic and environmental objectives will be forbidden under the MAI. While corporations are to be granted new rights and powers under the MAI, **they are to have no corresponding obligations and responsibilities related to jobs, workers, consumers, or the environment . . . .**

If this draft MAI is adopted by the OECD countries, the cornerstones of a new global economic constitution will be cemented in place. Even though the MAI will initially apply only to OECD signatory countries, an accession clause built into the proposed treaty allows non-OECD countries to sign into the pact, provided that certain conditions are met. This gives the U.S. the tools it needs to ensure that a 'high standard' investment treaty is established on a global basis without risking a watered-down version through prolonged negotiations under WTO . . . .

This new global constitution, however, is certainly not designed to ensure that the rights and freedoms of the world's people are upheld by democratically elected governments. On the contrary, **it is a charter of rights and freedoms for corporations only—a charter to be guaranteed by national governments in the interests of profitable transnational investment and competition.** It is meant to protect and benefit corporations, not citizens.

In effect, **the MAI amounts to a declaration of global corporate rule.** As such, it is designed to enhance the *political rights*, the *political power*, and the *political security* of the TNCs [transnational corporations] on a world-wide scale. . . .[9]

This guarantee of corporate dominance would totally obscure the non-profit work required for long-term survival and do nothing to promote employment opportunities for hundreds of millions of people who could be doing that necessary work and earning a living.

The MAI is an idea whose time must never come.

Addictive jobs

In a June 1997 referendum, Switzerland voted 80 percent in favour of continuing its profitable sale of weapons. The only reason—or excuse—offered in news reports was the need to avoid the loss of "good" jobs. To allow arms workers to put food on the family table, pay their mortgages and enjoy life, the Swiss voted to continue depending on the weapons business even if it pushes the troubled world closer to the brink of military madness.[10] It also happens in Canada. Witness the recent uproar over proposed closures of military bases.

Switzerland and Canada are by no means the only countries that are hooked on the deadly arms trade. Furthermore, weaponry is only one of many ways in which "good" jobs endanger the future for life on earth.

Right here in British Columbia the need for profits in forest industries, and the need for jobs among workers in forests and in lumber and paper mills, have caused governments to weaken many of the ecological regulations and services that had been intended to help in protecting our forests and the health of our planet. It seems to be either difficult or impossible for governments to make decisions for the long-range benefit of life on earth when the powerful voices of transnational corporations, elite economic think-tanks, and the dominant media all insist that economically we simply have no choice—that we must compromise the future of our planet and our society because we rely inescapably on unsustainable, unnecessary, and potentially catastrophic jobs.

As I continue to point out, however, there are other choices. There is plenty of necessary, beneficial work to be done. Unless such work can turn a profit, however, it has tended to be ignored by people who resist paying for such work through taxes, and who cannot imagine any other way to provide adequate financial support for non-profit work no matter how desperately it may be needed.

Funny business

In *Get A Life!* Wayne Roberts and Susan Brandum offer many examples of people outsmarting powerful, wealthy economic interests by creating for themselves exciting jobs in new, "fourth wave" businesses and lifestyles that are healthy, wealthy, and wise.

Among their principles for fourth wave economics, number 9 is "Easy Does It." The authors complain, "We've let the government and corporate turkeys create an employment problem which is worse than the unemployment problem. They get us working full-time on things that are wrong, while volunteers are left to put them right in their spare time."[11]

The book's subtitle emphasizes profit as an integral part of the eco-entrepreneurial dream: *How to make a good buck, dance around the dinosaurs and save the world while you're at it.* The title page suggests "One hundred and one ways to tread lightly on Mother Earth, make bags of money, simplify your life, have a blast, keep fit and save your sanity while everything is crumbling around you."

Principle number 5 borrows some wisdom from Jesse Jackson. "Anybody who would invest $40,000 to $60,000 a year to lock somebody up, rather than $6,000 to $8,000 a year to lift them up, is not using conservative economics."[12]

In some later edition perhaps the authors will apply their witty talents to identifying all the non-profit work required for a sustainable future and inventing some ingenious ways to pay for it.

Fair work and workfare

There have been societies where unemployment was unimaginable. They were once the norm. People of all ages did their part of the work of the community and everyone's needs were satisfied, including the need to be needed. Both hard times and good times were shared. In spite of hundreds of years of extreme pressure to change their ways and assimilate, many aboriginal societies still retain much of this fundamental heritage of sharing everything including resources, work, and respect, not only for each other but also for the land and for the next seven generations of life on earth.

Fair work has been well defined by the United Nations. On December 10, 1948 the General Assembly proclaimed the Universal Declaration of Human Rights.[13] Article 23 has four parts:

> (1) Everyone has the right to work, to free choice of employment, to just and favourable conditions of work and to protection against unemployment.
> (2) Everyone, without any discrimination, has the right to equal pay for equal work.
> (3) Everyone who works has the right to just and favourable remuneration ensuring for himself and his family an existence worthy of human dignity, and supplemented, if necessary, by other means of social protection.
> (4) Everyone has the right to form and to join trade unions for the protection of his interests.

Subsequently, in 1966, the General Assembly adopted the International Covenant on Economic, Social, and Cultural Rights.[14] Several articles in it explain what "fair work" should mean: "The States Parties to the present Covenant recognize the right to work, which includes the right of everyone to the opportunity to gain his living by work which he freely chooses or accepts. . . ."

In the Covenant, they

> recognize the right of everyone to the enjoyment of just and favourable conditions of work, which ensure, in particular:
> (a) Remuneration which provides all workers as a minimum with:
>   (i) Fair wages and equal remuneration for work of equal value without distinction of any kind, in particular women being guaranteed conditions of work not inferior to those enjoyed by men, with equal pay for equal work; and
>   (ii) A decent living for themselves and their families in accordance with the provisions of the present Covenant;
> (b) Safe and healthy working conditions;
> (c) Rest, leisure and reasonable limitation of working hours and periodic holidays with pay, as well as remuneration for public holidays.

They also recognize ". . . the right of everyone to an adequate standard of living for himself and his family, including adequate food, clothing and housing, and to the continuous improvement of living conditions. . . .[and] the fundamental right of everyone to be free from hunger . . ."

Furthermore, "Nothing in the present Covenant shall be interpreted as impairing the inherent right of all peoples to enjoy and utilize fully their natural wealth and resources."

That same year, 1966, the General Assembly also adopted the International Covenant on Civil and Political Rights[15] which proclaims that

> ... recognition of the inherent dignity and of the equal and inalienable rights of all members of the human family is the foundation of freedom, justice and peace in the world.
>   ... in accordance with the Universal Declaration of Human Rights, the ideal of free human beings enjoying civil and political freedom and freedom from fear and want can only be achieved if conditions are created whereby everyone may enjoy his civil and political rights, as well as his economic, social and cultural rights. . . .
>   All peoples have the right of self-determination. . . .
>   Every human being has the inherent right to life. This right shall be protected by law. No one shall be arbitrarily deprived of his life. . . .
>   No one shall be subjected to torture or to cruel, inhuman or degrading treatment or punishment. . . .
>   All persons deprived of their liberty shall be treated with humanity and with respect for the inherent dignity of the human person. . . .

Clearly, unemployment and underemployment are unacceptable. Now, what about workfare?

Workfare is a policy that requires welfare recipients to work in order to qualify for their social assistance cheques. This is most likely to be menial work with little or no pay, no "benefits", and no future. Workfare provides little or no training and little or no child care services. The workfare plan has failed to achieve its stated objectives in almost every Canadian province and American state where it has been tried. The only exception in reports I have seen is Massachusetts where the program is strictly voluntary and therefore should not even be called "workfare." [16] Every other North American workfare program denies welfare support to anyone who refuses to participate.

One thorough study of workfare experiences elsewhere was done by the Social Services Department of the Regional Municipality of Ottawa-Carleton. The study identified and challenged several basic assumptions made by all governments that have tried workfare:

- The evidence does not support the assumption that a large number of welfare recipients could find work if they wanted to, but choose to depend on welfare. That assumption ignores the fact of high unemployment. There is no substance to the argument that welfare payments and benefits are so high that they encourage welfare dependence. In fact, some workfare projects have denied basic help to people in genuine need, thereby contributing to the rapidly increasing dependence on food banks and soup kitchens.
- The assumption that the alleged cost of "widespread fraud" and "welfare cheats" could be eliminated by workfare is not justified. Abuse of the system is relatively low.
- The study also reported

> The assumption that workfare promotes self-sufficiency is hard to understand since self-sufficiency implies an absence of government assistance. Yet workers in workfare programs continue to receive their welfare payments. Workfare more often appears to reinforce dependency on the state, locking people into unskilled, make-work positions. . . . There is little evidence to support the assumption that workfare teaches new skills, offers training, and improves employability. Very few workfare participants are given work that involves meaningful training, and only a small percentage of those who complete such training programs find paying jobs. In New York, many workers in that state's workfare program have been performing the same entry-level job for nearly a decade.[17]

In Quebec the income security minister publicly admitted that workfare there has been a dismal failure. In the first five years of the program, the number of Quebecers on welfare increased by 42 percent! Of the 80 percent of welfare recipients considered "employable," only about 15 percent were actually enrolled in workfare programs as of 1996. Of those who did participate in such programs during the seven years since 1989, fewer than 12 percent were able to find stable jobs.

The cost of administering workfare in Quebec has been called "horrendous." A sociologist at the University of Montreal found that welfare agents had to spend 86 percent of their time doing financial work, such as "getting the right cheque to the right person at the right time," instead of doing more important casework services.[18]

Most analysts report that the main purpose served by workfare is to provide a pool of cheap labour for employers rather than help those on welfare or reduce welfare costs. Workfare workers have no right to join or to form unions, and are not covered by minimum labour standards legislation.

According to Robert Mullaly, social work professor at St. Thomas University in New Brunswick, workfare makes the business world and politicians happy. "Besides providing cheap labour and subsidizing employers, workfare takes jobs away from other workers and serves as a mechanism for keeping wages down and profits up."[19]

Workfare clearly violates the United Nations International Covenant on Economic, Social, and Cultural Rights which Canada signed, agreeing to "recognize the right to work which includes the right of everyone to the opportunity to gain his [her] living by work which he [she] freely chooses or accepts, and . . . take appropriate steps to safeguard this right."[20]

Workfare is no answer to unemployment. Fair work means genuine employment. That is what the United Nations General Assembly built into the Universal Declaration of Human Rights in 1948. Genuine employment is a major requirement of the 1966 International Covenant on Economic, Social, and Cultural Rights and it is protected still further in the 1966 International Covenant on Civil and Political Rights.

Leonard Marsh wrote the 1943 *Report on Social Security* in Canada on which Canada's post-war welfare program was based. Now he says, "The only answer to unemployment is employment—and not just any kind of employment, but employment carrying a reasonable level of remuneration and reasonably satisfactory working conditions."[21]

The Mondragon Worker Cooperatives

Dr. Frank Lindenfeld began his presidential address to the November 1996 meetings of the Association for Humanist Sociology in the U.S. with a blunt statement: "Corporate capitalism sucks." He pointed out that

> Major corporations poison our environment with toxic wastes, they market products known to be defective or even lethal, and they devastate communities through plant closings that idle thousands. How can they get away with this? In part because they fund politicians of both major parties who are in positions to protect their interests. Fifteen percent of the population—some 40 million Americans, including at least 16 million children—live in poverty, while wealth is increasingly concentrated in the hands of a small elite. The CEO of Coca Cola has accumulated nearly $1 billion in deferred compensation all by himself! [22]

The struggle to replace capitalism with a better system included the 1917 revolution by which the Russian Communist Party set up a state socialist economy. When people in central and eastern Europe were finally able to depose what had become a totally unacceptable Communist combination of socialism with the excesses of authoritarianism, their motto was "state socialism sucks!"[23]

Corporate capitalism and state socialism are both based on economic power concentrated in the hands of a small elite that is unaccountable to other people. In his speech Lindenfeld presented a third way, "The Cooperative Commonwealth—An Alternative to Corporate Capitalism and State Socialism."

Among Lindenfeld's several inspiring examples of consumer and worker cooperatives, one is so outstanding that it has been studied by interested visitors and scholars from many countries over the past half century.

It all began in 1941 at Mondragon in the Basque provinces of Spain after that region had been devastated by civil war. One of the soldiers in the Basque militia which failed to defeat the Fascist dictator Francisco Franco was a student priest called Jose Maria Arizmendi-Arrieta. He was captured by Franco's army and spent some time in gaol awaiting execution. Fortunately he escaped and returned to his seminary where he studied the Catholic social doctrine which rejected both the *laissez-faire* capitalism of Adam Smith and the revolutionary state collectivism of Karl Marx, and sought a third way that would achieve social justice while preserving individual property and freedom.[24]

Faced with deep poverty and massive unemployment in Mondragon, Don Jose Arizmendi started a technical school open to all local boys. He believed that "Knowledge was power—the key to a prosperous and classless society. The underprivileged must raise themselves by their own efforts." From the first graduating class, a dozen went on to become professional engineers. Five of them, poor working-class boys, obtained jobs in a metal factory. They tried to persuade the boss to allow increased worker participation, but management refused, citing the need to protect the rights of shareholders.

In their frustration the five started their own factory in 1956. They consulted Father Arizmendi and decided on a cooperative structure. It is remarkable that the Mondragon network of worker cooperatives remains strong forty years later and twenty years after the death in 1976 of Don Jose Maria Arizmendi-Arrieta. Although this Mondragon system still considers itself "experimental" and subject to revision, it employs about 30,000 workers in a network which includes industrial, agricultural, business, educational, housing, and banking cooperatives. It services over 100,000 people in four of the seven Basque provinces.[25]

According to Lindenfeld, this collectively owned cooperative system has reached such a size and scale that "we can begin to talk about its becoming a credible challenge to capitalist institutions." In the early 1990s the network reorganized itself as the Mondragon Cooperative Corporation (MCC).[26]

George Benello's book, *From the Ground Up: Essays on Grassroots and Workplace Democracy*, concludes that

> Mondragon is worth studying because it works, and the
> argument can be made that utopian theory must always
> confront the practical since the burden of proof is on
> the theorist. The problem with capitalism and, more
> generally, with coercive industrial systems of whatever
> persuasion, is not that they don't work; they do deliver
> the goods, but in the process grind up human beings.
> The only answer to this state of affairs is to prove that a
> better system also works; theory alone simply will not
> do.[27]

Arizmendi-Arrieta's vision brought a group of cooperatives together as early as 1959 to create a financial base for their enterprise. Caja Laboral Popular (CLP), the Working People's Bank, is not only the bank for all Mondragon cooperatives but is itself a workers' cooperative.

The CLP made it possible to strengthen existing cooperatives and finance new ones. As of 1993 Mondragon included 176 cooperatives: 96 industrial, 8 agricultural, 4 service sector, 46 educational, 1 retail, 15 housing, and 6 support. ("Support" means co-ops of co-ops, including the CLP, the insurance division and research and technology.)[28]

The CLP is a financial and investment institution whose resources have increased from millions of dollars in 1965 to billions in the 1990s. Through the CLP, money derived from the cooperatives stays within the region where it can be used to benefit the whole community as well as the individual workers and their cooperatives.

Monthly salaries are based on the level of job responsibility required for each position, but no one can receive more than six times the lowest salary in the Mondragon system. In earlier decades the maximum difference was only three to one. Even with that severe cap on higher salaries, the Mondragon cooperatives were able to attract an excellent body of highly educated and skilled people for top level work.

Every worker in the system is a member and every member is a worker. In order to join, a worker must invest $4,000. Anyone who does not have enough money can borrow what is needed from the CLP on favourable terms, like a mortgage to buy a house. By investing in the cooperative system every worker has a personal stake in its continued success and expansion.

At least 10 percent of the annual surplus or profit is allocated to a social, educational, and charitable fund for projects benefiting the community.

Another 20 percent goes into a collective, reserve fund which cannot be claimed by members if the cooperative breaks up. That prevents members with a market advantage from selling out to realize large gains. If the surplus is higher than normal the percentage for the reserve fund is increased. If, instead, there are losses, they are shared by members.

The collective fund makes it possible for the CLP to provide capital needed by individual cooperatives and for the development of new cooperatives. Instead of allowing any one cooperative to get too big it may be subdivided into units of a healthier size.

The remainder of the surplus, normally 70 percent, is credited to the value of shares held by individual members. These cannot be reclaimed until the member leaves the cooperative or retires.

The supreme authority in the MCC is the annual meeting of the general assembly with one vote for each member. Practical responsibility throughout the year is delegated to a managing board elected from the membership.

Under Spanish law, members of the cooperatives were considered to be self-employed and not eligible for the State social security benefits. In response the CLP set up another second-degree cooperative to fill that gap, providing health insurance, workers' compensation, pension plans, and medical services to members.[29]

Cooperatives have to conduct all their banking with the CLP which has the right to audit them every four years. The bank has an entrepreneurial division that helps to create cooperatives and also provides consulting services and emergency assistance to existing cooperatives. Its main role is to finance the creation, expansion and well-being of worker cooperatives and other cooperative organizations.[30]

A cooperative student factory was founded to allow students to participate in both study and work, helping them to pay their way and get practical, apprenticeship experience at the same time.[31]

Back in 1981 Dominic Flassati wrote that Mondragon cooperatives gained a competitive edge over capitalist businesses by the fact that 90 percent of all profits are retained in the firm— as either individual or collective capital.

> In the recession now hitting Spain [in 1981], Mondragon has not sacked a single worker. If workers become redundant, they are sent back to the Technical College for advanced training in subjects like automation. When business picks up, they may go back to their factory. If not, they will be found jobs in a new co-op starting up in a more profitable field.[32]

In 1983 Robert Gilman wrote *Mondragon: The Remarkable Achievement.* In his view the most important achievement might be that

> . . . they have healed the split between labor and management/ownership, thereby allowing much more balanced and wholistic decision making. Consider what happens in our system when a plant fails to produce the profit expected of it. The owners look at the situation purely in terms of the return on capital, and if they could get a better return elsewhere, they may well close the plant. The investments the workers have in their community and all the social costs of the closing do not enter into the accounting of the relative profitability of keeping the plant open.
>
> In the Mondragon system, all these factors are considered. The Mondragon worker-owners are not sentimental and they will not tolerate a non-performing business, but when a cooperative runs into trouble, they are willing to put out the extra effort to find a new and better way. If it means lower income and lower profits for a while, they—as workers and owners, the business and the community—are willing to put up with it. They

can make hard choices much more creatively and with more balance than those who are locked into adversarial roles.[33]

Many books and articles about Mondragon are filled with wonder and enthusiasm. In recent years, however, critics have noted some dimming in that golden glow.

The Myth of Mondragon by Sharryn Kasmir was the first critical account of this internationally renowned, leading, alternative model to standard industrial organization. Even though these cooperatives are considered to be the most successful examples of democratic decision making and worker ownership, Kasmir argues that the enthusiastic literature on Mondragon idealizes the cooperatives by incorrectly portraying them as apolitical institutions and ignoring the actual experiences of workers. She thinks this glowing picture of an ideal system is part of a new global ideology that promotes cooperative labor-management relations in order to discredit labor unions and working-class organizations. Previous studies had examined the cooperatives mainly from managers', not workers' perspectives. She calls this the "myth" of Mondragon.[34]

Frank Lindenfeld is critical of Eroski, a growing chain of consumer cooperatives. It is the fastest growing part of the MCC, setting up "more and more supermarkets including the giant size ones or hypermarkets. Hundreds of co-op markets now provide employment for some 10,000 persons." He wrote,

> The MCC seems to have successfully met the challenge of the integration of Spain into the European Common Market, but there are signs it is wavering from its cooperative principles. The investments of the Caja no longer exclusively promote cooperative development. Moreover, as the retail network continues its breakneck expansion, its democratic features are in danger of being watered down. One issue is the hiring of non-member workers, whose numbers appear to be growing. Another relates to annual membership meetings. Because of the large numbers involved, network members no longer meet together in a general assembly of the whole. Rather,

they meet in different geographical regions to choose
delegates who in turn elect the Board of Directors.[35]

David McMullen wrote,

> While the cooperatives put some thought into developing
> advanced forms of management and work organization,
> they do not appear to be better in this regard than the
> more 'enlightened' private corporations. The main value
> of Mondragon would appear to be in showing how it is
> possible for cooperatives to operate in large scale modern
> industry.

McMullen asks whether worker cooperatives foster rebellion against
the present system or collaboration with it? "Obviously," he says,
worker cooperatives should never be seen as an ultimate objective.
They still involve market relations, and these breed exploitation,
and economic crisis and stagnation." McMullen suggests that
industrial democracy and worker cooperatives may

> reflect a real world dilemma. On the one hand change
> requires rebellion and defiance against those who would
> exploit us and squeeze our lives into little boxes. On the
> other hand it requires the development of an experience
> based understanding of how to run things ourselves.
> To put it more graphically, rebellion by surly but stupid
> slaves is not the basis of radical change.[36]

A 1993 Economic Justice Report says that the people of
Mondragon "still call what they are doing a social and economic
experiment. Can they run the co-ops more democratically? Do
women have an equal role to men in the co-ops? Are environmental
concerns being sufficiently met?"[37]

I have not seen any evidence that the Mondragon system has
paid any special attention to our unprecedented global predicament
as it has been documented, for example, in the *World Scientists' Warning
to Humanity*. If Mondragon cooperatives are aware and concerned
about our "drift toward unparalleled catastrophe," are

they considering any changes in their "modes of thinking" or ways of doing business to respond effectively to such a warning?

Even acknowledging these unanswered questions and some negative criticism, democratic worker ownership through two generations at Mondragon has demonstrated remarkable achievement and suggests great promise for a world now approaching a new century in deep social, economic, and ecological trouble.

"Natural Capitalism"

When I first saw these two words together, I wondered about them. In combination do they not constitute an oxymoron? However, Paul Hawken's analysis of "natural capitalism" in his *Mother Jones* article under that name is anything but oxymoronic.[38] He focusses on that "capital" which is absolutely essential for life on earth, natural capital.

"Everyone," he wrote,

> is familiar with the traditional definition of capital as accumulated wealth in the form of investments, factories, and equipment. 'Natural capital,' on the other hand, comprises the resources we use, both nonrenewable (oil, coal, metal ore) and renewable (forests, fisheries, grasslands). Although we usually think of renewable resources in terms of desired materials, such as wood, their most important value lies in the services they provide. These services are related to, but distinct from, the resources themselves. They are not pulpwood, but forest cover, not food but topsoil. Living systems feed us, protect us, heal us, clean the nest, let us breathe.

Paul Hawken says these living systems "are the 'income' derived from a healthy environment: clean air and water, climate stabilization, rainfall, ocean productivity, fertile soil, watersheds, and the less appreciated functions of the environment, such as processing waste—both natural and industrial."

Natural capital has been largely ignored in business planning. Up until the 1970s there seemed to be so much of it available that there was no point counting it. Most economists have considered manufactured capital the main factor in industrial production— money, factories, etc. Natural capital has been seen throughout the industrial era as just a marginal factor, but now it must become our first priority.

We have experimental evidence that

> there are no man-made substitutes for essential natural services. We have not come up with an economical way to manufacture watersheds, gene pools, topsoil, wetlands, river systems, pollinators, or fisheries. Technological fixes can't solve problems with soil fertility or guarantee clean air, biological diversity, pure water, and climatic stability; nor can they increase the capacity of the environment to absorb 25 billion tons of waste created annually in America alone.

When the industrial era began there were plentiful resources and fewer people. Now natural resources are diminishing while human population is escalating exponentially. Economist Herman E. Daly cautions that

> we are facing a historic juncture in which, for the first time, the limits to increased prosperity are not the lack of man-made capital but the lack of natural capital. The limits to increased fish harvests are not boats, but productive fisheries; the limits to irrigation are not pumps or electricity, but viable aquifers; the limits to pulp and lumber production are not sawmills, but plentiful forests.[39]

Together with these inescapable warnings, Paul Hawken also offers realistic hope. "Like all previous limiting factors, the emergence of natural capital as an economic force will pose a problem for reactionary institutions. For those willing to embrace the challenges of a new era, however, it presents an enormous opportunity."

Instead of firing perfectly capable people only to allow corporate employers to "wring out one more wave of profits," he says, we now have an opportunity to employ even more people to devise and carry out ways to conserve natural capital. We need capable people working to reduce the unnecessary, wasteful overuse of "unproductive kilowatts, barrels of oil, tons of material, and pulp from old-growth forests."

When 1 billion willing workers can't find a decent job or any employment at all, Hawken insists, "Clearly, we need to make fundamental changes." He quotes William Strickland's experience in work with troubled children and youth: "You can't teach algebra to someone who doesn't want to be here." He refers to children who do not want to be here, anywhere at all, alive, on earth. No one is listening to them, so they *demand* our attention through high risk behaviour, like unprotected sex, drugs, violence—and, finally, outright crime (or suicide).

We respond by wasting more money, building more jails, employing more police, lawyers, judges. This does nothing to overcome the root causes of alienation and agony for children and youth. Like accidents, oil spills, earthquakes, and floods, these attempts to control youth behaviour do actually raise the GDP, the Gross Domestic Product, but not the quality of life for children, youth or adults. The GDP is just a measure of the amount of money changing hands—for better or for worse.

Paul Hawken does not hesitate to advocate bold, daring changes:

> We have to revise the tax system to stop subsidizing behaviors we don't want (resource depletion and pollution) and to stop taxing behaviors we do want (income and work). We need to transform, incrementally but firmly, the sticks and carrots that guide business. ... To create a policy that supports resource productivity will require a shift away from taxing the social 'good' of labor, toward taxing the social 'bads' of resource exploitation, pollution, fossil fuels, and waste.

In spite of daunting obstacles, Hawken is hopeful "because the solution is profitable, creative, and eminently possible:"

> You can win a Nobel Prize in economics and travel to the royal palace in Stockholm in a gilded, horse-drawn brougham believing that ancient forests are more valuable in liquidation—as fruit crates and Yellow Pages—than as a going and growing concern. But soon (I would estimate within a few decades), we will realize collectively what each of us already knows individually: It's cheaper to take care of something—a roof, a car, a planet—than to let it decay and try to fix it later.[40]

Do we still have "a few decades" left for public learning before we drift into "unparalleled catastrophe?"

Volunteerism

Volunteers do a prodigious amount of important work now. Could that service be extended somehow to take on all the non-profit or third-sector work required for survival and well-being?

Municipal and other governments might be persuaded to support third-sector work financially, at least in part, because failure to do this work will be even more expensive than helping to pay for it. For example, it will cost more to keep a person in prison than to increase the kind of work that could help to reduce crime and thus diminish the alleged need for so much legal and prison expense.[41]

In *Love in a Cold World?* Dr. Paul LeDuc Browne reports on his study of "The Voluntary Sector in an Age of Cuts." Although he writes mainly about the Canadian experience under a policy of severely reduced funding for public services, most of his findings seem to have some general application around the world.

A majority of voters and legislators have been sold in recent decades on cutting the size of government. *Laissez-faire* is the classical liberal/conservative economic doctrine of minimal government interference in the market. Let the market operate according to its ownTF intrinsic principles, they say, because "State interference with this natural order, even when motivated by the noblest of intentions, can only be counter-productive, undermining the work ethic, discouraging investment, slowing economic growth and increasing poverty."

To achieve the greatest economic growth and increase the amount of wealth available to all, neo-conservatives believe that each individual must try to maximize his or her own profit in the marketplace. In order to "free enterprise," it is necessary to attack the welfare state.

> This means restricting government control of business as much as possible, by reducing corporate taxes, environmental regulations, labour standards, employment equity, rules over the use of urban and rural space, regulations governing financial institutions and transactions, as well as limitations on trade and investment. It therefore also entails lessening the protection the welfare state affords workers, whether through legislation (labour standards, union rights) or social programs (unemployment insurance, workers' compensation, pensions, medicare, etc.).[42]

To take the place of a dismantled welfare state, charitable organizations and community groups are expected to bear much heavier responsibility for humanistic services.

Acknowledging that government debt cannot be ignored, Browne takes exception to "current policies [that] are less about reducing debt than transferring wealth from the public to the private sector, and from the less well off to the better off."[43]

> The problem . . . is that most non-profit organizations are too small, too locally-based, have too little money and too few employees, and are too dependent on government funding, to be able to play more than a very modest role in providing social security in the event of government cutbacks.[44]
> . . . voluntary organizations require adequate, stable, reliable funding in order to accomplish their missions in an orderly and coherent fashion.[45]

Under neo-conservative, corporate rule, supported by revolting taxpayers, he says, funds have been severely cut for non-governmental organizations as well as for government services. Many organizations that have been advocating for health, full employment, education, human rights, environmental protection, and peace and justice in Canada and around the world have been categorically dismissed as "special interest groups," not deserving of public funds or even support from private sources.

Many not-for-profit organizations are helped by having charitable status which allows their private donors to receive tax benefits. "However," Browne writes, "in the free-for-all of competing fund-raising campaigns, the larger organizations, which can hire professional fund-raisers and mobilize more volunteers, will likely reap disproportionate benefits from their charitable status."[46]

Browne cautions that, "Given the increasing use of volunteers in various public services, . . . great care must be taken that employability programs promoting volunteering do not become a vehicle for substituting the free labour of volunteers for the remunerated labour of public sector workers."[47]

It is a deplorable fact that the increasing reliance on volunteers is beginning to displace paid public sector workers, even teacher aides, library aides, clerical workers, receptionists, porters, laundry workers, and emergency reception assistants.

> . . . volunteers do not appear so much to be helping to bridge the gap during a period of austerity, as in fact to be facilitating cuts. Yet volunteers do not have to meet the same standards of performance as paid employees, nor do they face the same attendance requirements. . . . Women are more affected by this trend than men, because volunteers are usually deployed in jobs that are more often held by women. This undermines women workers' bargaining power, and therefore their prospects of achieving pay parity. 'Employers are quite willing to replace women on low pay with women on no pay.' . . . The replacement of paid staff by volunteers leads to declining standards and morale in the workplace.[48]

"There are alternatives," he writes,

> although they get little airing in the mainstream media—
> for example using the Bank of Canada to lower interest
> rates and take on a much larger share of the debt;
> investing in job creation; redistributing working time;
> introducing new taxes on wealth and financial
> transactions. . . . It is possible to envisage ways of
> reforming the welfare state other than subordinating it
> to the unfettered rule of market forces.[49]

Browne's concluding chapter shows that much valuable but
neglected knowledge is stored in experienced grassroots workers,
unemployed and underemployed people, poor people, elderly and
differently abled people, aboriginal people, and other minorities.

> Social movements and voluntary organizations form a
> dense social fabric which provides invaluable resources
> for democratic life. . . . But if the voluntary sector and
> social movements produce social capital on the margins
> of a world ruled entirely by market forces and
> considerations, then all their efforts may not amount to
> more than love in a cold world, palliative measures for
> those most hurt or least able to cope.

Instead of being treated as passive recipients of diminished
services, all these people must be included as active participants in
planning and changing needed services and workplaces.

The ultimate goal, Browne says, must be to transform civil society
and build full-fledged democracy at both local and national levels.

> The social and labour movements and a democratized
> state are complementary: only the latter can maintain a
> political, economic and cultural environment in which
> civil society can thrive, while only the social movements
> can generate the mass mobilization necessary to
> democratize the state. It is no coincidence that both face
> the same enemy today in the ideology of neo-
> conservatism and those who propagate it.[50]

In the next chapter we shall turn to other sources for some very realistic advice on what it will take to overcome—or get around—that "same enemy", elite control, which already dominates in most countries and is well on its way to dominance throughout the world.

"Turning 2000"

Volunteer work does have strong advocates and much merit if it is used appropriately. Laurie Gourlay, with his partner, Jackie Moad, developed this voluntary concept as far back as 1985. Their brochure reminds everyone that

> The turn of the century is just around the corner. A powerful moment in history, a time to honour past efforts and to celebrate, the new millennium will also be a time to look ahead.
>
> There is much we can do as individuals, and together, to foster a better world for our children and the generations to come.
>
> The hardships and wars faced by our parents, and those before them, need never occur again. By giving something of ourselves, as they did, we can pass on the promise and opportunities of a better future.
>
> One hour a month, to the community organization of your choice, can make a world of difference.
>
> A little effort now will reap lasting rewards. Giving our time, working together for a better future, offering to help our communities develop for the good of us all—this is a heritage we can proudly pass on.
>
> The example is ours to set.[51]

When we multiply one hour a month by billions of human beings the product will be a huge number of volunteer hours every year. Even this modest amount of dedicated service per volunteer can accomplish a significant amount of good work.

On December 31, 1996, The Turning 2000 Project offered $2000 in prizes and seed money to local projects, for the best ideas to make the world a better place in the new millennium!

All around the world millions of individual and organizational volunteers are trying to help sustain the planet and restore health and well-being to life in each community on earth. "Turning 2000 requires a commitment from individuals to pledge 12 hours to improve their community. Every year until 2015 the volunteer will be asked to renew that pledge so that over 30 years roughly 360 hours of community work will be dedicated by each participant." [52]

In March 1997, to celebrate 25 years of action, *World Inter-Action Mondiale* published its first newsletter with a message from President of the Board of Directors Laurie Gourlay. He wrote,

> In these times it takes extra effort and strong convictions to speak up for others less fortunate the world 'round. . . . Though universal rights, freedom and equality have not come easily to many countries of the world, and have still to be fought for in far too many places, still the world is a better place for our efforts. And so it is that we approach the millennium, with time yet to foster that new world we've been dreaming of. [53]

Waging Peace for a Living

Many valuable ideas are underway or in the works for increased employment doing important work for the benefit of life on earth. We need all of these entrepreneurial efforts and then some. I think we also need to include WAGING PEACE FOR A LIVING when people on earth undertake to transform our modes of thinking and our ways of living for the twenty-first century.

Notes

1. "The Turned-on People," *Look* Magazine, New York: June 28, 1966, pp. 33-36. This photographic article includes a short piece about Dr. Richard Farson, Dr. Carl Rogers and others involved in exciting, leading-edge human developments of the 1960s in California.

2. Angus Reid, *Shakedown: How the new economy is changing our lives*, Toronto: Black Sturgeon Enterprises, published in Canada by Doubleday Canada, 1996, pp. 293-294.

3. *Ibid.*, pp. 297-298.

4. Dr. William Krehm, Chairman, Committee on Monetary and Economic Reform, "A Creative Solution to Debt and Taxes" in *The Networker*, Toronto: COMER Publications, 3284 Yonge Street, Suite 500, Toronto, Ontario M4N 3M7, Issue #4, 1995.

5. Bruce O'Hara, *Working Harder Isn't Working: How we can save the environment, the economy and our sanity by working less and enjoying life more*, Vancouver: New Star Books, 1993.

6. Bruce O'Hara, "The Case for Working Less: Four-day work week key to healthy economy" in *CCPA Monitor*, Ottawa: Canadian Centre for Policy Alternatives, November, 1995, p. 1.

7. Walt Taylor, "The Case for Working More: Jobs scarce, but plenty of work to be done" in *CCPA Monitor*, Ottawa: Canadian Centre for Policy Alternatives, March, 1996, p. 18.

8. Scott Nova and Michelle Sforza-Roderick, an article in *The Nation* which first reported the leaked information about secret negotiations in Paris for MAI, Multilateral Agreement on Investment, New York: early 1997.
   The authors are Director and Research Associate at the Preamble Collaborative/Preamble Centre for Public Policy, Washington, D.C.

9. Tony Clarke, "MAI-day! The Corporate Rule Treaty," Ottawa: published by Canadian Centre for Policy Alternatives, April, 1997, pp. 1, 2.
   This 12-page essay is "A Preliminary Analysis of the Multilateral Agreement on Investments (MAI) which seeks to consolidate global corporate rule."

10. CBC Radio News, 1998.

11. Wayne Roberts and Susan Brandum, *Get A Life! "How to make a good buck, dance around the dinosaurs and save the world while you're at it,"* Toronto: Get A Life Publishing House, October, 1995, p. 261.

12. *Ibid.*, p. 153.

13. The Universal Declaration of Human Rights declared by the General Assembly of the United Nations in New York on December 10, 1948.

14. The International Covenant on Economic, Social, and Cultural Rights adopted by the General Assembly of the United Nations in New York, 1966.

15. The International Covenant on Civil and Political Rights adopted by the General Assembly of the United Nations in New York, 1966.

16. "Workfare a failure everywhere it's been tried: An Administrative Nightmare," in *CCPA Monitor*, Ottawa: published by Canadian Centre for Policy Alternatives, July/August 1996, pp. 20-21.
    This article is based on material provided by *Labour Times*, *This Magazine*, The Canadian Union of Public Employees, and the Regional Municipality of Ottawa-Carleton.

17. *Ibid.*, p. 20. Quotation from the in-depth study of workfare by the Social Services Department of the Regional Municipality of Ottawa-Carleton.

18. *Ibid.*, p. 20.

19. *Ibid.*, p. 21.

20. *Op. cit.*, Note 14.

21. *Op. cit.*, Note 16.

22. Dr. Frank Lindenfeld, "The Cooperative Commonwealth—An Alternative to Corporate Capitalism and State Socialism," Presidential Address to the November 1996 meetings of the Association for Humanist Sociology, Hartford, Connecticut, p. 1.
    He is a professor at Bloomsburg University in Pennsylvania.

23. *Ibid.*, p. 1.

24. Dominic Flassati, " Viva la co-operativa! A Spanish success story," *New Internationalist*, December 1981, p. 12-13.

25. "Mondragon, Spain—The 'Experiment' that Endured," from Economic Justice Report, April 1993 in the CUSO "Common-Sense Economics" Ideas Bank Index.

26. *Op. cit.*, Note 22, p. 4.

27. Colin Ward's review, p. 3, of C. George Benello's *From the Ground Up: Essays on Grassroots and Workplace Democracy*, Boston: South End Press, 1992. www.nothingness.org/sociala/sa20/20ward.html

28. *Op. cit.*, Note 25.

29. Bob Milbrath, "Lessons from the Mondragon Coops," in *Science for the People*, May/June, 1983.

30. David McMullen, "Taking a closer look at Workers' Control," from www.su.sin.edu.au/~davidm/pages/worker.htm, p. 5.

31. *Ibid.*, p. 5.

32. *Op. cit.*, Note 24, p. 14.

33. Robert Gilman, "Mondragon: The Remarkable Achievement," originally published In *Context* #2, Spring 1983, Copyright 1983, 1996 by Context Institute, p. 44.
from www.context.org/ICLIB/ICO2/gilman2.htm, p. 5.

34. Sharryn Kasmir, *The Myth of Mondragon: Cooperatives, Politics, and Working-Class Life in a Basque Town*, Albany: State University of New York Press, 1996.

35. *Op. cit.*, Note 22, p. 4,5.

36. *Op. cit.*, Note 30, pp. 5,6.

37. *Op. cit.*, Note 25, p. 2.

38. Paul Hawken, "Natural Capitalism," in *Mother Jones*, March/April 1997, pp. 39-54.

39. *Ibid.*, p. 42-46.

40. *Ibid.*, p. 50-62.

41. *Op. cit.*, Chapter 3, Note 6(a).

42. Dr. Paul LeDuc Browne, *Love in a Cold World? The Voluntary Sector in an Age of Cuts*, Ottawa: Canadian Centre for Policy Alternatives, 1996, pp. 18,19.

43. *Ibid.*, p. 72.

44. *Ibid.*, p. 20.

45. *Ibid.*, p. 51.

46. *Ibid.*, p. 57.

47. *Ibid.*, p. 40

48. *Ibid.*, pp. 62, 63.

49. *Ibid.*, p. 73.

50. *Ibid.*, pp. 82-89.

51. Laurie Gourlay, "Turning 2000," a collection of letters, brochures, announcements, inviting people to contribute one hour each month to some organization of their choice working for a better world. Material is dated from 1986 through 1997. Address: Turning 2000 Project, Box 175, Station A, Ottawa, Ontario K1N 8V2.

52. "Canada: Turning 2000," an announcement, June 1990.

53. *Inter-Action*, Newsletter from World Inter-Action Mondiale, March 1997. Address: 180 Argyle Street, Ottawa, Ontario K2P 1B7.

"*I'm absolutely against total war, but then I'm not for total peace, either.*"

危机 CHAPTER 10

Transforming Deadly Nightmares into Living Dreams

> Optimism is essential for life even when it may not seem justified by the available evidence.
> —Taylor's Law

In this "turnaround decade" we face not one, but two extreme dangers. While responding to the ecological threats to our planet and its life presented in Chapter 1, the whole world must also defend itself now against the surprisingly rapid shift in our society away from democratic government for all people toward corporate rule by and for a powerful and increasingly affluent minority.

The English word "crisis" is represented in the Chinese language by two characters: one for "danger" and the other for "opportunity."[1] With our eyes opened wide to the ecological and dictatorial *dangers* built up during the twentieth century, the conclusion of this chapter will focus on available *opportunities* for us to foster the survival and well-being of life on earth in the twenty-first.

Our occupied planet

In the darkest days of the genocidal Holocaust, when a brutal Nazi dictatorship occupied most of Europe, tortured and massacred millions of human beings, and nearly extinguished democratic life on earth, many people living in the midst of these atrocities excused themselves later, saying: "We didn't know. We didn't see a thing. We didn't hear the victims' screams."

A minority of people did see what was happening and felt the pain. Many of them joined together in a risky, underground resistance movement. They took secret action together in a courageous attempt to undermine dictatorship and restore hope for some degree of democracy.

Dr. Ursula Franklin is a distinguished professor of metallurgy at the University of Toronto who has also been a lifelong activist for peace and justice. She wrote,

> I have been in this game too long, written too many briefs and been on too many delegations to Ottawa to be sanguine about saying, 'The poor dears need some more knowledge. If they only knew what I know, the world would be a better place to live.'
>
> One begins most of these civic journeys with the idea that those in power are well-intentioned but ill-informed, and I am sorry to say that many of us ended up by saying that those in power are very well-informed but ill-intentioned.
>
> They (the politicians) have no intention of doing what I might consider the right and appropriate thing.[2]

In a 1997 speech she delivered to a Ten Days for Global Justice seminar in Toronto, Dr. Franklin said,

> I find the current situation bearable with the help of two things. One is a concept of the reality in which we live, and the second is a look back at history.
>
> I picture the reality in which we live in terms of military occupation. We are occupied the way the French and Norwegians were occupied by the Nazis during World War II, but this time by an army of marketeers. We have, as the occupied nations of Europe had, puppet governments who run the country for the benefit of the occupier. We have, as they did, collaborators.
>
> We, like the French and Norwegians at the time, have to protect our families and so are forced on occasion to

work with the occupiers to survive. Like the citizens of Nazi-occupied Europe, however, we must develop strategies for building a resistance movement. We have to reclaim our country from those who occupy it on behalf of their global masters, who have only contempt for those whose territory they now rule.

The goal of the occupiers is privatization, which, in its most brutal terms, means to provide investment and profit opportunities in all those areas that people previously had set aside as common holdings—culture, health care, education, publishing, housing, nature, sports, prisons. Once dismantled, the 'public sphere' can be more easily 'occupied'—turned over to what I call the Empire of the Marketeers. These warlords will convert the ill-health and misery and basic needs of our neighbours into investment opportunities for the next round of global capitalism.[3]

The urgent need for this resistance movement is thoroughly documented in Tony Clarke's 1997 book, *Silent Coup*. He presents a challenging but workable resistance plan in the second half of the book, justifying its bold subtitle, *Confronting the Big Business Takeover of Canada*. The desperate need and an appropriate action plan go far beyond Canada, however, to confronting the "Big Business Takeover" of the world.

Clarke thinks that mobilizing for action requires genuine hope for the future:

> If people are going to commit themselves to a resistance movement they need to know that they are fighting for something.
>
> An alternative vision of the future, in other words, is an essential part of any struggle for democratic social change. Yet the public is constantly being fed a heavy dose of TINA—There Is No Alternative—by the country's business and political elites. This, of course, is simply a form of intellectual terrorism. There *are* alternative options which should be a vital part of public discussion and debate in a democratic society.

> The strategy of selling TINA is based on the politics of fear, which in the end is anti-democratic. But what this means, in effect, is that people not only need to know that alternatives exist; they must also believe these alternatives are viable and achievable if they are going to commit themselves to a prolonged struggle to make them a reality.[4]

Two fundamental instruments for realistic hope could be the WORK INVENTORY and the FINANCIAL SUPPORT INVENTORY opening the way for a viable alternative, WAGING PEACE FOR A LIVING.

"Indeed," Clarke declares,

> the time is ripe! All across the country today [and around the world?] there are increasing signs that the politics of insecurity are alive and well. Stubbornly high levels of joblessness, massive layoffs from corporate downsizing (including governments), along with the dramatic shift from full-time to part-time employment, have created a climate of growing *economic insecurity* for many Canadians. The relentless wave of cutbacks in government funding for health care, public education, social assistance, post-secondary education, and unemployment insurance has greatly heightened levels of *social insecurity*, particularly among women. On top of all this, there is an increasing sense of *ecological insecurity* among Canadians, who fear what will happen as governments reduce environmental regulation, cut back on the monitoring and enforcement of pollution standards, and make it easier for mining, forestry, and energy corporations to speedily extract and export our non-renewable natural resources.
>
> The theme running through all of this insecurity is a fear that people are losing control over their economic, social and ecological future. In turn, this fear is intensified by the growing awareness of the extent to which corporations now control their political as well as their economic and social welfare. When deepening class divisions are added, this politics of insecurity becomes a potentially volatile mixture.[5]

Is there any light at the end of this tunnel? "In the midst of all this upheaval," he observes,

> some rays of hope may be detected. After all . . . the system of corporate rule has been built on shaky foundations, economic as well as political. So much so that its built-in contradictions could intensify to the point where major political cracks may soon appear. Take, for example, the casino economy in which investment has become a game for gamblers and speculators. The trillions of dollars in cyber-money transferred around the world every day have inflated a financial bubble that could well burst if not controlled in the near future by some kind of global financial sector regulation.
>
> Or take the industrial sectors of the economy, which have deployed new technologies to produce a massive supply of goods and services, but cannot sell them because of inadequate consumer demand and purchasing power.
>
> Consider, too, the signs of anxiety and uncertainty now surfacing among some CEOs [chief executive officers of corporations] and their political and academic allies. Until recently, they extolled the merits of unrestricted international competitiveness and foreign investment as the foolproof tools for building a prosperous global economy. Now they are beginning to see that the free market religion is not delivering the economic Utopia its high priests had promised.
>
> Add to these first cracks in the corporate rule structure the rumblings of social unrest generated by the inequality and insecurity it has spawned, and we can find reasons to believe that the reign of the business overlords may not be as absolute and as long-lasting as they intended it to be. Even if it does not collapse from its internal stresses and contradictions, the corporate New World Order is surely vulnerable to community-based resistance focused on its weakest elements.[6]

Clarke warns that this "task of national reconstruction will be a long and arduous struggle. It will require a revitalization of political will and a restoration of public confidence." He says this "long-term plan of action . . . could well take the next 10 to 15 and perhaps 20 years to accomplish."[7]

Do we still have 20 years left before we drift, as Einstein worried half a century ago, into unparalleled catastrophe? Recall that senior world scientists declared in 1992 that "No more than one or a few decades remain before the chance to avert the threats we now confront will be lost and the prospects for humanity immeasurably diminished."[8] The resistance movement for national and international reconstruction must get moving!

Making compost

All these dire warnings will be wasted if we simply ignore them. We must not let that happen. These warnings contain a lot of good stuff. We shall compost these twentieth century nightmares into fertilizer to provide rich nourishment for our twenty-first century dreams and to bring them to life.

Composting will begin by translating the alarming scientific details of worsening dangers to the planet and its life into a catalogue of the specific work that must be done to respond to dangers and to take full advantage of opportunities. The evidence of corporate rule will be composted into the necessary public motivation and energy to build an international resistance movement to construct a new society based on democratic principles, ecological economics, and an aboriginal type of respect for Planet Earth and her remarkable, but nevertheless finite, carrying capacity. All this work will be included in the WORK INVENTORY for all communities in all countries to consider.

A parallel composting process will explore areas of wasted wealth on Planet Earth in order to locate sufficient funds for top priority, non-profit work that is not being done now even though it is absolutely necessary for the future of life on earth. Not only too many people, but also vast amounts of money, are either unemployed or underemployed in the great struggle for the well-being of life and for a healthy survival of the planet, itself. This second phase of composting will prepare the FINANCIAL SUPPORT INVENTORY, a catalogue of innovative ways to provide sufficient funds to pay for doing all the work in the WORK INVENTORY.

Les Miserables of recent centuries will not have suffered in vain when we learn from their pain how to spread respect, sharing, compassion, responsibility, justice and realistic hope around the world.

When to begin?

During the summer of 1974 I had the privilege of working in British Columbia with Nazko and Kluskus First Nations people who were troubled by plans for a logging road that would cut right through the heart of their traditional territory and split in two their principal community, Nazko Village, near Quesnel, British Columbia. They were not fundamentally opposed to logging, but they wanted to be included in the planning process and have their community interests considered. They developed some good ideas for harvesting logs in the area without disrupting their cultural life or destroying the regional habitat. For example, they offered some unusual proposals for "roadless logging," possibly using blimps.

When this thoughtful, generous, innovative report was completed before the tight deadline which had been imposed on it by government officials, the Nazko and Kluskus people put a heartfelt message into the conclusion of their work. They said, "THE FUTURE IS NOW!" [9]

Chief Dennis Patrick wrote, "That's a problem with the Indian Movement. We don't take action. We wait for the government to do things for us. We should just go ahead and do it ourselves. When we have ideas, good ideas, we wait for the government to say yes or no. The Future Is Now. The basic thing we are trying to do is to get a better future for our people."[10]

An effective action plan should have begun at least fifty years ago, but the next best time to start after that is NOW. There is no time like the present to begin drafting the necessary inventories for full and challenging employment doing all the non-profit work required for a promising future. If we fail to change very soon our "modes of thinking," our global direction, we shall end up where we are now heading—toward unparalleled catastrophe.

Where to Start?

In Chapter 4, I suggested that it could begin in some forward-thinking, non-governmental organization or coalition. However, that is by no means the only place the resistance movement could start.

It could start in one or more universities. It could certainly flourish with imaginative collaboration among students and faculty. Scholars could begin translating the dire scientific warnings of the twentieth century into a catalogue of the work required to respond effectively in the twenty-first century.

It might be launched from a spaceship one day while a group of astronauts contemplate together the unprecedented predicament of life on earth from their extraordinary perspective above it all.

It could get underway with a consortium of scientific and human rights organizations brought together, perhaps, by the Union of Concerned Scientists, the organization that coordinated the 1992 *World Scientists' Warning to Humanity.*

Or, to consider yet other possibilities, WAGING PEACE FOR A LIVING—or some other, superior action plan—might be conceived and hatched around a kitchen table, possibly even in your town.

What stands in the way?

All kitchen table groups that are dedicated to the survival and well-being of life on earth for the next seven generations will face certain inescapable challenges. The obstacles to making necessary paradigm changes in our thinking and our ways of living seem so daunting that many concerned people may experience them as nightmares. However, confronting these obstacles openly will make it possible to take a second, more determined look.

1. The immense size of the Waging Peace project is one obstacle. Every community has a backlog of work that needs to be done right there at home, but *each region must also give serious thought to doing its share of necessary global work.* That means work that must be done, even though it is largely non-profit work, that no region or country can do all by itself without cooperative participation from many other regions.

2. Two powerful forces promote endless economic growth. One is the pressure of world population that has at least tripled in the twentieth century and is still growing exponentially while the landbase and resources available to serve the needs of life on earth is actually shrinking. The other is the assumption, especially in rich, industrialized countries, that economic growth is necessary, regardless of its cancerous impact on earth.

3. The chasm between rich and poor people is already vast and getting even wider. Our global society cannot long endure such a gross division between outrageous wealth far beyond the earth's carrying capacity and abject poverty which threatens not only health, but even life itself.

4. Complacency stands in the way. Somewhere in between the extremes of wealth and poverty, too many of us are relatively and temporarily comfortable, like the frog in a pan of cool, but warming water. We are too comfortable just now to "change our modes of thinking," even in response to dire warnings. We do not feel sufficient pressure to worry about our accelerating "drift toward unparalleled catastrophe." However, if we wait until the water around us gets much closer to boiling, it will be too late to jump!

5. Many relatively comfortable working people have to consider more immediate dangers than any dire, but seemingly distant, global warnings. They must "pay the mortgage" for sure, and

some may have to worry about possibly losing a job. In forestry, agriculture, fishery, mining, government service or other occupations, it can be difficult to give serious thought to more ecological ways of doing your job when your pay depends on satisfying the boss.

Unemployed and underemployed people face plenty of challenges to personal or family survival without putting much of their limited resources and energy into the struggle for survival of life on earth.

6. Too many of us are still confident that science and technology will eventually overcome all obstacles to the survival and well-being of life on Earth. However, we dare not ignore some disastrous side effects of increasingly powerful science and technology while basking in their beneficial achievements.

Only yesterday we learned from the work of Albert Einstein that $E=mc^2$. Then we produced atomic bombs and actually dropped them on two cities, killing or disabling many thousands of men, women and children. We landed on the moon and now we are already exploring Mars with a serious plan to establish a colony there, perhaps as soon as the twenty-second century. Even that ingenious plan, however, requires that we get the necessary work done to sustain life on Earth until Mars is ready—at least seven generations hence.

7. Under corporate domination, the mainstream media stands in the way of adequate public awareness of both danger and opportunity. Without fully comprehending the unprecedented crisis of our day, we can neither see clearly where we are nor plan wisely what to do. For now we have to depend heavily on spreading more widely the information and exchanges of wisdom found in some excellent alternative media.

To circumvent all these obstacles will require uncommon cooperation. For example, in order to combine their individual strengths into an effective struggle for survival and well-being, non-governmental organizations will have to find ways to agree on plans, resolve differences, and select able coalition leaders while maintaining enthusiastic appreciation of all leaders and other participants whose cooperation will enhance NGO collaboration. Working together as a team, NGOs will need to appreciate and support each organization's individual projects while, at the same time, putting their collective strengths into an ambitious, cooperative response to global dangers and opportunities.

Where to find the money to prepare the inventories?

We know there is plenty of money in the world to do what must be done, but how can a sufficient amount be secured and allocated now to this urgent purpose, preparing the first drafts of the WORK INVENTORY and the FINANCIAL SUPPORT INVENTORY?[11] For a full year of well-paid, hard work by two teams of researchers, you will find a draft budget in Appendix III. The main challenge is to gain public recognition that these inventories deserve top priority. Once we have done that, the funds will be available.

However, we do not have either the time or the money to convince the whole world of this urgent need. That is why I proposed in Chapter 7 that a coalition of NGOs provide a small working group for waging peace. That working group could invite half a dozen able and already convinced volunteer researchers to put their heads, hearts, and hands together for a year to prepare these draft inventories. Some interested non-governmental organizations might each second a staff member to assist in this first step toward WAGING PEACE FOR A LIVING.

Even with enthusiastic volunteer help, however, a reduced but still substantial budget will be necessary for all the other expenses.

Breathing life into a dream

Once we have these inventories in hand, we will be able to demonstrate their usefulness in several interested communities or regions. Demonstrations will be especially appropriate and illuminating in regions where unemployment is high and people are so desperate for paid work that they will continue fishing even when fish stocks are in danger of extinction and continue cutting and milling more trees than the forests can stand to lose. Hoodwinked by the canard that there really is no alternative to such deadly jobs, these workers see no other way to put food on the table and pay the mortgage.

The best way to prove that there are good alternatives is to put examples on display in a great variety of experimental regions. We desperately need these regional demonstrations that there are, in fact, magnificent alternatives. Full and challenging employment for everyone on earth is one priceless alternative worthy of an unprecedented global information campaign. There is plenty of rewarding, non-profit work that must be done and there is wealth enough to allow all those who do this work to earn a respectable living.

We must escape from that oft-repeated excuse for endangering the future of life on earth, the widespread myth of TINA, "There Is No Alternative!"[12] It is pure propaganda, financed and spread by corporate interests whose bottom line it serves.

Maybe that cool, comfortable water in which we are temporarily basking is getting warm enough now to suggest that we take a bold, quantum leap, before it is too late, into some very exciting and enticing alternatives. WAGING PEACE FOR A LIVING is certainly one alternative. It includes the fascinating work required for a paradigm switch to *ecological economics* and to *natural capitalism*.

Much to gain; little to lose—even for affluent folks

Even wealthy people, affluent shareholders and chief executive officers of profitable transnational corporations, can have nightmares. Many corporate leaders lose sleep just imagining any serious drop in unemployment. High unemployment helps to keep unions under control; it keeps wages down and profits up.

Far beyond any financial worries, however, wealthy people must also pay close attention to the *World Scientists' Warning*. It applies to them as members of humanity who depend for life support on keeping our endangered planet healthy.

If we continue the way we are going the richest people will have the most to lose—everything! Even billionaires have children and grandchildren whose survival and well-being are precious. Wealthy families also require food, clean air and water, education and health maintenance. They need protection against stratospheric ozone depletion, species loss, deforestation, global warming, violence, crime, human rights violation, and war. Omnicide and terracide endanger rich as well as poor people.

When increasing numbers of people start making fundamental changes in our modes of thinking, our ways of living, and our ways of earning a living, affluent people as well as all others will have much to gain. Wealthier people will have opportunities to move away from what might be called an alienated minority seeking ever more personal wealth and to fit comfortably into a cooperating majority seeking higher quality for all life on earth.

John Levy of the Jung Institute coined the name for a disease that afflicts many wealthy people. He called it *affluenza*. The symptoms in children include "boredom, low self-esteem, and lack of motivation" which result, he suggests, from "the family wealth that insulates children from challenge, risk, and consequence." Referring to *affluenza*, Marion Edelman, President of the Children's Defense Fund, spoke about a *New York Times* report that "psychologists and psychiatrists are finding parallels between children of the urban rich and poor. They both suffer from broken homes and absentee parents. . . . Both move around easily accessible drugs, alcohol and sex."[13]

Poverty and *affluenza* are two malignant diseases which could both be virtually eradicated by skillfully mixing an increase in employment for underemployed workers with excellent use of some underemployed wealth to support the workers financially.

"Sustainability," wrote Bill Rees and Mathis Wackernagel, "will have a hard sell until we can show that people have more to gain than to lose by changing their ways."[14]

Who will gain when WAGING PEACE FOR A LIVING provides full employment doing work that is necessary for the planet and its life? The gains will be significant and the losses trivial for everyone: poor people, rich people, those in between, all other life on earth, our planet herself, and possibly our galaxy.

Impossibility and necessity

When I was young we knew, because it was so obvious, that setting foot on the moon was impossible. Now, of course, it has actually been done. In *Valuing the Earth,* economist Herman Daly described "impossibility statements" as "the very foundation of science." Some things really are impossible and always will be. For example, he says, it is impossible to travel faster than the speed of light, to create or destroy matter-energy, or to build a perpetual motion machine.[15]

Before undertaking any challenging project it is helpful to know whether it is impossible or not. It would be futile and foolish to waste time and resources on a project that simply cannot succeed.

Some endeavours, so difficult that they *seem* impossible at first, are actually *necessary*, the very opposite to impossible. One project that provides the main theme in *Valuing the Earth* is the need to replace our impossible dependence on endless economic growth with an understanding, at last, that we can and must switch to economics without growth—ecological or "steady state" economics.[16]

However, ever since 1987 when the Brundtland Report emphasized "sustainable development", those have become the predominant global buzz words.[17] Herman Daly thinks that

> economists should be very interested in impossibility theorems, especially the one to be demonstrated here, namely that it is impossible for the world economy to grow its way out of poverty and environmental

degradation. In other words, sustainable growth is impossible.

In its physical dimensions the economy is an open subsystem of the earth ecosystem, which is finite, nongrowing, and materially closed. As the economic subsystem grows it incorporates an ever greater proportion of the total ecosystem into itself and must reach a limit at 100 percent, if not before. Therefore its growth is not sustainable. The term 'sustainable growth' when applied to the economy is a bad oxymoron—self contradictory as prose, and unevocative as poetry.[18]

Daly uses the dictionary to distinguish between growth and development.

To grow means 'to increase naturally in size by the addition of material through assimilation or accretion.' *To develop* means 'to expand or realize the potentialities of; to bring gradually to a fuller, greater, or better state.' When something grows it gets bigger. When something develops it gets different. The earth ecosystem develops (evolves) but does not grow. Its subsystem, the economy, must eventually stop growing, but can continue to develop. The term 'sustainable development' therefore makes sense for the economy, but only if it is understood as 'development without growth'—i.e., qualitative improvement of a physical economic base that is maintained in a steady state by a throughput of matter-energy that is within the regenerative and assimilative capacities of the ecosystem. Currently the term 'sustainable development' is used as a synonym for the oxymoronic 'sustainable growth.' It must be saved from this perdition.[19]

When introducing "The Nature and Necessity of the Stationary State," Daly credits John Stuart Mill and quotes at length from his 1857 essay, *Principles of Political Economy*. Seven generations ago, Mill "spoke of the stationary state in words that could hardly be more relevant today."[20] He wrote:

I cannot . . . regard the stationary state of capital and wealth with the unaffected aversion so generally manifested towards it by political economists of the old school. I am inclined to believe that it would be, on the whole, a very considerable improvement on our present condition. [written in 1857!] I confess I am not charmed with the ideal of life held out by those who think that the normal state of human beings is that of struggling to get on; that the trampling, crushing, elbowing, and treading on each other's heels which form the existing type of social life, are the most desirable lot of human kind, or anything but the disagreeable symptoms of one of the phases of industrial progress. The northern and middle states of America are a specimen of this stage of civilization in very favorable circumstances; . . . and all that these advantages seem to have yet done for them (notwithstanding some incipient signs of a better tendency) is that the life of the whole of one sex is devoted to dollar-hunting, and of the other to breeding dollar-hunters.

. . . I know not why it should be a matter of congratulation that persons who are already richer than anyone needs to be, should have doubled their means of consuming things which give little or no pleasure except as representative of wealth. . . . It is only in the backward countries of the world that increased production is still an important object: in those most advanced, what is economically needed is better distribution, of which one indispensable means is a stricter restraint on population.

. . . Nor is there much satisfaction in contemplating the world with nothing left to the spontaneous activity of nature; with every rood of land brought into cultivation, which is capable of growing food for human beings; every flowery waste or natural pasture plowed up, all quadrupeds or birds which are not domesticated for man's use exterminated as his rivals for food, every hedgerow or superfluous tree rooted out, and scarcely a place left where a wild shrub or flower could grow without being eradicated as a weed in the name of improved agriculture. If the earth must lose that great portion of its pleasantness which it owes to things that the unlimited increase of wealth and population would extirpate from it, for the mere purpose of enabling it to support a larger, but not a happier or a better population, I sincerely hope, for the sake of posterity, that they will be content to be stationary, long before necessity compels them to it.

It is scarcely necessary to remark that a stationary condition of capital and population implies no stationary state of human improvement. There would be as much scope as ever for all kinds of mental culture, and moral and social progress; as much room for improving the Art of Living and much more likelihood of its being improved, when minds cease to be engrossed by the art of getting on. . . .[21]

Is the "steady-state economy" (SSE) left or right? Herman Daly points to the one thing that socialism and capitalism have agreed upon. They formed an unfortunate consensus that economic growth is necessary. Both socialism and capitalism reject the idea of a SSE. "Both systems," Daly says, "suffer from growthmania, and the SSE presents as much a challenge to Big Socialism as to Big Capitalism. But it also offers a point of reconciliation for the future. When old adversaries discover that they have made the same error, their brotherhood in humility should facilitate reconciliation."

To identify either growth or steady state with either left or right would be a mistake because that would

obscure the emergence of a third way, which might form a future synthesis of socialism and capitalism into a SSE and eventually into a fully just and sustainable society. Neither capitalism nor socialism can make much of a claim to being just, sustainable, and participatory. Let us not insist on pouring new wine into old wineskins.

. . . it is more profitable to work out the concept of steady state, of a just and sustainable society, as a third way—neither capitalistic nor socialistic but a way to which traditional capitalists and socialists are invited to contribute and within which they might find an embracing synthesis.[22]

Hope and beyond hope toward confidence

The Responsible Wealth project and the organization that spawned it, United for a Fair Economy, justify some new hope for change in powerful, affluent modes of thinking. If members of Responsible Wealth succeed in their educational campaign, and if enough people who are not wealthy develop a parallel resistance movement, I think we may be able to advance during the opening decades of the new century and millennium *beyond hope to a measure of outright confidence in the future.*

This book opened with an invitation to "Abandon despair, all ye who enter here." A quarter century ago, while Boyce Richardson was well on his way to becoming a distinguished Canadian writer, he and I had a long discussion about optimism and pessimism.[23] We were both in Montreal where we shared a terrible sadness over the failure of Cree and Inuit people and their supporters to prevent the social, economic, and cultural devastation threatened by the James Bay Hydro Project's occupation of aboriginal territory. Toward the end of our talk, Boyce Richardson accused me of "unquenchable optimism."

After some years, that conversation led me to a personal proclamation of "Taylor's Law". I must confess that I have witnessed and experienced so much regional and global discouragement over the years that I often find myself depending heavily on Taylor's Law:

> OPTIMISM IS ESSENTIAL FOR LIFE EVEN WHEN IT MAY NOT SEEM JUSTIFIED BY THE AVAILABLE EVIDENCE.

It is difficult to sustain unquenchable optimism in a world where maximizing private profit takes precedence over peace with justice, and where elected politicians are manipulated under corporate rule like so many puppets. Pessimism creeps in when "realistic" wars make huge profits for a few while action to promote peace and a fair distribution of the world's wealth is scorned as wild-eyed, Utopian dreaming. Cynicism gains a foothold when massive unemployment is treated as just a necessary expense of doing business as usual. How can we justify hope when mainstream economists, the media, elite financial interests, political leaders, and even many employed and unemployed workers are all brainwashed into agreeing that "there is no alternative" to everlasting economic growth even though it is taking us right to the brink of terracide and omnicide?

Governments have cut deeply into our customary social safety nets because they were considered far too expensive—even health care, education, unemployment insurance, and social welfare. When trying to imagine some creative ways to respond to unprecedented global warnings, we are cautioned not even to think "beyond our means." "Be sure to keep our dreams within budget limits," we hear. "Stay the course" in order to reduce the deficit, pay off the debt, control inflation and balance the budget—"come Hell or high water!"

As we near the end of this "turnaround decade," most people have never heard of the *World Scientists' Warning to Humanity*. Very few responsible, influential people are even aware of it and no adequate, responsive action is yet in sight. Nearly 1700 of the world's most distinguished scientists have become merely frustrated, unheard voices crying in the wilderness while even the wilderness is rapidly disappearing.

What can we possibly *do* about such overwhelming dangers?

It is not just a few revolting taxpayers, wealthy speculators, and elite investors who worry about the high cost of restoring health to our planet and protecting the future for life on earth. We are all so completely inundated by propaganda from the military-corporate complex that *most of us* assume, without specifically saying so, that we simply cannot *afford* survival and well-being for Mother Earth and all the life which depends on her!

As a matter of fact, however, millions of deeply concerned people are at work right now in thousands of dedicated organizations around the world, all struggling in one way or another to change our modes of thinking and open the way for the survival and well-being of life on earth.

Realistic idealism

A CRISIS, as Chinese linguists know well, is when DANGER and OPPORTUNITY come together. People like myself, who anticipate increasing public enthusiasm for an ambitious action plan for survival and well-being of life on earth are sometimes called "dreamers."

However, when we dare to look these ugly, turn-of-the-millennium dangers right in the eye, and we start taking full advantage of some extraordinary opportunities that we hardly ever noticed before and have not yet fully appreciated, it may begin to seem possible for many dreams to come alive after all.

Those of us who look forward to a mutually beneficial cultural exchange between the indigenous people who came here first and their powerful neighbours who arrived later are sometimes considered naive.

Nevertheless, among the alternatives already slowly emerging, there is an improvement in cross-cultural hearing and vision. One-way, imposed assimilation is fading, for example, after 500 years of newcomers occupying the aboriginal homeland throughout the Americas. The wit, wisdom and spirit of indigenous people around the world is beginning to be more widely recognized and appreciated, even though there is still a long way to go and much work to be done.

I do agree that our endangered world desperately needs vigorous, collaborative opposition to many prevalent ways of thinking and ways of living that are not only inappropriate, but also put at risk our continued existence and the health of the earth on which we totally depend.

At the same time it seems clear that opposition is not enough. It will not be good enough just to concentrate on what we should not do and what we should *stop doing*.

It will be at least equally important to identify and begin actually implementing alternatives which will not only sustain immediate hope for people of all ages around the world, but also justify an increasing level of confidence in the health of life on earth for the next seven generations.

When WAGING PEACE FOR A LIVING—or some other action plan—demonstrates opportunities for full employment actually doing urgently needed work, then insecure workers will no longer feel a need to cling to employment that is socially damaging, ecologically threatening and economically unsustainable. They will have superior alternatives to consider!

At the end of the day and near the end of the millennium, I believe the time has now arrived when idealism has finally become realistic and anything much short of idealism is no longer practical.

Notes

1. See the two Chinese characters for CRISIS on the cover and in the frontispiece.

2. Dr. Ursula Franklin, "Futile Lobbying" in *CCPA Monitor*, Ottawa: Canadian Centre for Policy Alternatives, March 1997.

3. Dr. Ursula Franklin, "Canada under the occupation of an army of marketeers," in *CCPA Monitor*, Ottawa: Canadian Centre for Policy Alternatives, July/August 1997, pp. 22-23.
   Dr. Franklin is a retired professor of metallurgy, a Quaker, a peace activist, and member of the Voice of Women. This article was adapted from a speech she delivered at the Ten Days for Global Justice Seminar in Toronto, February 1, 1997.

4. Tony Clarke, *Silent Coup: Confronting the Big Business Takeover of Canada*, Ottawa: Canadian Centre for Policy Alternatives and Toronto: James Lorimer and Company, 1997, p. 174.

5. *Ibid.*, p. 177.

6. *Ibid.*, pp. 177-178.

7. *Ibid.*, p. 205.

8. *World Scientists' Warning to Humanity*, sponsored by the Union of Concerned Scientists, Two Brattle Square, Cambridge, Massachusetts 02238-9105, December 1992.

9. The Nazko-Kluskus Study Team, "Report to Nazko and Kluskus Bands of Carrier Indians," Nazko Village, British Columbia: August 17, 1974.

10. Nazko Chief Dennis Patrick, "The Future is Now!" in Coyoti Prints: Caribou Tribal Council Newsletter, Vol. III Number 9, Williams Lake, British Columbia: special Nazko-Kluskus edition, published at Fish Lake Cultural Education Centre, September 20, 1976.

11. *Op. cit.*, Chapter 6, Note 4.

12. *Op. cit.*, Note 4.

13. Marion Wright Edelman, "Who's Watching the Children?" Wheaton College Commencement address, Norton, Massachusetts, May 21, 1988.
Marion Edelman spoke as President of the Children's Defense Fund, Washington, D.C.

14. *Op. cit.*, Chapter 1, Note 16, p. 137.

15. *Op. cit.*, Chapter 5, Note 2. See "Sustainable Growth: An Impossibility Theorem" by Herman E. Daly, p.267.

16. *Ibid.* See Herman E. Daly's "Introduction to Essays Toward a Steady-State Economy," pp. 11-47, plus the entire book.

17. *Op. cit.*, Chapter 1, Note 32 (m). See Chapter 2, "Toward Sustainable Development," pp. 43-66.

18. *Op. cit.*, Chapter 5, Note 2, p. 267.

19. *Op. cit.*, Chapter 5, Note 2, pp. 267-268.

20. *Op. cit.*, Chapter 5, Note 2, p. 27.

21. *Op. cit.*, Chapter 5, Note 2, pp. 27-28.

22. *Op. cit.*, Note 15. See pp. 376-377 in Chapter 20, "Postscript: Some Common Misunderstandings and Further Issues Concerning a Steady-State Economy."

23. Boyce Richardson, *Strangers Devour the Land: The Cree Hunters of the James Bay area versus Premier Bourassa and the James Bay Development Corporation*, Toronto: The Macmillan Company of Canada, 1976.
See also Boyce Richardson's early films: "Job's Garden" and "Cree Hunters of Mistassini" for examples.

危机 EPILOGUE

Seven Reasons for Cautious Optimism on Entering the Twenty-first Century

> Our task must be to free ourselves . . . by widening our circle of compassion to embrace all living creatures and the whole of nature in its beauty.
> —Albert Einstein

The best news of the twentieth century is that its worst news is finally leaking out. Now we can begin looking danger right in the face and taking full advantage of opportunity.

In his 1995 book, *When Corporations Rule the World*, David C. Korten says that we have come to a crisis in history where we must rethink the very nature and meaning of human progress. He underlines Herman Daly's compelling message: Sustainability is utterly impossible in a globalized economy that demands everlasting economic growth.

After declaring that continuing on our present course will lead to "accelerating social and environmental disintegration," Korten expresses optimism:

> It is within our means, however, to reclaim the power that we have yielded to the institutions of money and re-create societies that nurture cultural and biological diversity—thus opening vast new opportunities for social, intellectual, and spiritual advancement beyond our present imagination.[1]

The greatest barrier to our genuine progress is the limited extent of public awareness that our world has become dominated by a small but extremely powerful minority of financially elite individuals and corporations.

Instead of merely *leaking out* to the public, however, the information we so urgently need will soon begin breaking out all over—like Spring! As more people become fully aware of the catastrophic dangers confronting us at the end of the twentieth century, we shall discover great opportunities for changing our obsolete modes of thinking in order to accommodate the requirements of the twenty-first century.

Consider at least the following seven reasons for enough optimism to inspire our necessary quantum leap into waging peace:

1. Vibrant coalitions expand public awareness

PGA is not well known—yet. Following a conference in 1998, People's Global Action emerged as a network of grassroots movements from around the world.

The New Internationalist described it in a November 1998 article by Katherine Ainger, "Intelligent graffiti, hysterical police." The PGA manifesto declares, "Despite the huge material differences, struggles in privileged and underprivileged parts of the corporate empire have more and more in common, setting the stage for a new and stronger sort of solidarity. . . . Scattered around the world again [after the conference], we will not forget. We remain together. This is our common struggle."

PGA is planning many events in Europe for May and June 1999. "Several hundred activists from all over the world will come together to demonstrate in European cities, including Geneva, Paris, Cologne, Brussels, London." The timing of this action will coincide with the regular G8 summit of financially elite countries in Cologne.

Katherine Ainger called it ". . . a dramatic statement of global protest from the coalitions of the dispossessed to the world policy-makers, bankers and transnational corporations." In her view, ". . . the champions of global capitalism are already on the defensive."

People's Global Action promises to become a landmark display of global resistance and solidarity. Susan George (Director of the Amsterdam-based Transnational Institute) says: "Not since the Vietnam War have I seen a movement come together like this." [2]

*   *   *

The Hague Appeal for Peace will convene from May 11 to 15, 1999, in The Hague, Netherlands. On the 100th anniversary of the first Hague Peace Conference of 1899, hundreds of non-governmental organizations and thousands of activists from all over the world will gather to create and launch The Hague Agenda for Peace and Justice—a global action plan for the 21st Century.

This last major conference of the century is organized by civil society but it seeks to involve three key sectors—people, international organizations, and governments—in delegitimizing war and promoting a culture of peace.

A number of key issues will be integrated into the campaign. These include: a focus on gender, the concerns of indigenous peoples, the role of the media in armed conflict, the effect of globalization on regional peace and security, the environment, religion, peace education, and youth perspectives and participation. There will be four program strands:

1. International Humanitarian and Human Rights Law and Institutions.

2. Prevention, Resolution, and Transformation of Violent Conflict. "The twentieth century has proven that, left to their own devices, governments are not very good at preventing, resolving or transforming violent conflict. If the mistakes of this century are to be avoided in the next, we must ensure that a strong system of people's diplomacy takes its place alongside the diplomatic efforts of governments."

3. Disarmament, Including Nuclear Abolition.

4. The Root Causes of War—A Culture of Peace. "This Program
   Strand will examine the following underlying or 'root' causes of
   conflict:
   > Poverty and economic inequalities
   > Ethnic and religious conflict and nationalistic movements
   > Environmental degradation and the scarcity/misallocation of
   > natural resources
   > The marginalization of indigenous populations including the
   > persistence of colonialism
   > The role of the media in perpetuating violence
   > The absence of democratic institutions of global governance
   > The failure to protect all human rights, including civil,
   > political, environmental and socio-economic rights"[3]

*   *   *

In Latin America the term "neo-liberalism" is commonly applied
to the prevailing system in which a powerful, affluent minority
maintains "liberal" policies which enrich the already wealthy and
impoverish, control, and oppress the majority.

In reports from other parts of the world I often come across
two terms, "neo-liberal" and "neo-conservative." In my own
understanding, I can see no real difference between them. Both
continue to widen still further the existing vast chasm between
extreme wealth and influence far beyond the earth's tolerance and,
on the other side, abject poverty and powerlessness.

In 1998 "The Peoples' Summit" brought together some 1,000
men, women and children from nearly every nation of the
hemisphere to Santiago, Chile. They focused on building a
hemispheric social alliance around some concrete, viable alternatives
to neo-liberalism.

The courageous optimism of this assembly can be fully
appreciated only by recalling the bloody beginning of neo-liberalism
in Chile on September 11, 1973, when elected President Salvador
Allende was murdered and his democratic government brutally

smashed by Augusto Pinochet's coup, with covert backing by United States military power. While many hundreds of Chilean people were made to "disappear" or suffer during years of political imprisonment, torture, and slaughter, the Pinochet dictatorship invited U.S. economists from the University of Chicago to introduce new rules for Chilean economic development that were in line with the interests of those who financed the coup, rules that were enforced by state-sanctioned terror.

A reason for cautious optimism in this context is the growing public awareness of problems together with an exploration of promising solutions as published in the 1999 book, *Alternatives for the Americas: Building a Peoples' Hemispheric Agreement.* In this report of an extraordinary international cooperative effort, the assembled people expressed their collective rejection of dominant policies that promote trade and investment liberalization, deregulation, privatization, and market-driven economics as the formula for development, when that formula has been disastrous for most peoples of the hemisphere.

Not far from the "Peoples' Summit," the presidents and prime ministers of these nations were also meeting in Santiago to launch the negotiation of a Free Trade Area of the Americas (FTAA), scheduled for completion in 2005. It is expected to follow the pattern of existing agreements like NAFTA, expanding neo-liberalism still further throughout the hemisphere.

At the opening of FTAA negotiations in Santiago, U.S. President Clinton proclaimed Chile as "the model for the hemisphere." This praise reveals the intent of the most powerful government of the Americas to use the FTAA to promote an extreme form of neo-liberalism. By contrast, Luis Anderson, President of the Interamerican Regional Workers' Organization (ORIT), stated at the Peoples' Summit the very next day: "When young children must come and beg for food, we must be clear that Chile is no model!"

The main questions raised by people at the summit are: Whose rules will prevail, and who will benefit?

The Preface to *Alternatives for the Americas* is rich with information needed for public awareness: ". . . Throughout the hemisphere, there is a stratum of society that is doing very well by neo-liberal policies. The speculators, the transnational corporations, and those in their service proclaim the wonders of the market. But for most of us, the past 25 years have meant declining living standards and in many cases abject poverty." [4]

With cautious optimism, this peoples' report goes far beyond negative criticism of past horrors to stimulate further debate and education for a superior alternative vision for the future.

2. A closed door opens

On December 2, 1998, Dr. Joseph Gosnell, chief negotiator for the Nisga'a Nation, and his associates were welcomed as honoured guests into the Legislative Assembly of the Province of British Columbia in Canada.

Chief Gosnell addressed the members of the Legislative Assembly:

> . . . In 1887 my ancestors made an epic journey from the Nass River to here, Victoria's Inner Harbour. Determined to settle the land question, they were met by a Premier who barred them from this Legislature. He was blunt. Premier Smithe rejected all our aspirations to settle the land question. Then he made this pronouncement: 'When the white man first came among you, you were little better than wild beasts of the field.' Wild beasts of the field. Little wonder, then, that this brutal racism was soon translated into narrow policies which plunged British Columbia into a century of darkness for the Nisga'a and other aboriginal people. . . .
> . . . the situation of the Nisga'a worsened. In 1927, Canada passed a law to prevent us from pursuing our land claims, from hiring lawyers to plead our case. At the same time, our central institution of tribal government, our potlatch system we know in Nisga'a as *ayuuk*, was outlawed by an act of Parliament. It was against the law for us to give presents during our

ceremonies, which is central to our tradition; our law instructs us to do that. It was made illegal for us to sing and dance, which again is a requirement of our culture. But still we did not give up, and finally, under the leadership of Dr. Frank Calder, the Nisga'a Land Committee was reborn as the Nisga'a tribal council in 1955. . . .

How the world has changed! Two days ago and 111 years later, after Smithe's rejection, I walked up to the steps of this Legislature as the sound of Nisga'a drumming and singing filled the rotunda. To the Nisga'a people it was a joyous sound—the sound of freedom. Freedom is described in the dictionary as 'the state of being free, the condition of not being under another's control, the power to do, say or think as one pleases.' Our people have enjoyed the hospitality and the warmth of this Legislature, this capital city, its sites and its people. In churches, schools and malls, streets and public places our people have been embraced, welcomed and congratulated by the people of British Columbia. . . .

To us a treaty is a sacred instrument. It represents an understanding between distinct cultures and shows a respect for each other's way of life. We know we are here for a long time together. A treaty stands as a symbol of high idealism in a divided world. That is why we have fought so long and so hard. I have been asked: 'Has this been worth it?' I would have to say, with a resounding yes, it has. . . .

We are not naive. We know that some people do not want this treaty. We know that there are naysayers—some sitting here today. We know that there are those who say Canada and British Columbia are giving us too much, and a few who want to reopen negotiations in order to give us less. Others, still . . . are practicing a wilful ignorance. This colonial attitude is fanning the flames of fear and ignorance in this province and reigniting a poisonous attitude that we as aboriginal people are so familiar with.

But these are desperate tactics, doomed to fail. By playing politics with the aspirations of aboriginal peoples, these naysayers are blighting the promise of the Nisga'a treaty not only for us but for non-aboriginal people as

well, because this is about people. We're not numbers.
The issue that you will deal with over the next weeks [is]
the lives of our people, the future of our people. It is
about the legitimate aspirations of our people, no longer
willing to step aside or be marginalized. We intend to be
free and equal citizens. . . .

Now, on the eve of the fiftieth anniversary of the
Declaration of Human Rights, this Legislature embarks
on a great debate about aboriginal rights. The Nisga'a
people welcome that debate, one of the most important
in the modern history of British Columbia. We have
every confidence that elected members of this
Legislature will look beyond narrow politics to correct
the shameful and historic wrong. I ask each and every
one of you, honourable members, to search your hearts
deeply and to allow the light of our message to guide
your decisions.

We have worked for justice for more than 100 years.
Now it is time to ratify the Nisga'a treaty, for aboriginal
and non-aboriginal people to come together and write a
new chapter in the history of our nation, our province,
our country and, indeed, the world. The world, I believe,
is our witness to the endeavours that we have
encountered.

Madam Speaker, on behalf of the Nisga'a nation, I
greatly appreciate the privilege that has been accorded
to me to address this chamber. Thank you." [5]

3. A demonstration of sustainable forestry

Merv Wilkinson has proven by his own work over the past fifty
years that it is possible to harvest a small forest continually while
enriching the soil at the same time, encouraging wildlife, increasing
the amount and safety of employment, substantially improving the
quality of the trees, and passing on to future generations a sustainable
opportunity for earning a good living in harmony with the rest of
nature.

His remarkable way of operating a successful tree farm while
caring for the earth was documented in a small book in 1990,
Wildwood: A Forest for the Future by Ruth Loomis with Merv
Wilkinson.[6]

By telephone at the beginning of 1999 I learned from Merv Wilkinson that he is well into his eighties and still working his forest. He just completed his thirteenth cut. With one minor exception, the media have given his good work fair and adequate coverage. He is pleased by progress in sustainable forestry in such countries as Costa Rica, Nepal, Columbia, Mexico, United States, Malaysia and Borneo. Wilkinson's practical demonstration of forest enrichment may some day be recognized and adopted in his own country, Canada.

Susan Zwinger's 1994 interview with Wilkinson could serve as an excellent introductory course in profitable and beneficial forest stewardship. A few extracts from the interview will illustrate just a little of the wisdom he has gained from his practical experience:

> My 136 acre "Wildwood" is a sustained-yield, selectively logged tract of timber that has produced forest products since 1945, and will continue to do so as long as it is taken care of. Here the forest is growing faster than I log it. Without destroying the forest, I harvest trees periodically for specialized products and regularly for lumber. We are enjoying the forest in its tranquility; all living organisms are present and healthy.
>
> I grew up on the edge of a natural forest, knowing that we are part of the forests. Yet they are here to use. To enjoy. They can be maintained. They should never, never be destroyed. If we are to have any forests left in the next fifteen years, it is absolutely necessary that we stop our clearcutting. . . . I do not want to be around when the last forest is gone. . . .
>
> Yes! Eight or nine rings per inch is about average of this property which is a very high quality of wood. That is done by forcing the tree to grow up, not out. Again by the fact that you're just removing individual trees, so creating only small gaps in the canopy. No tree likes to have a tree taller than itself. Trees are very, very competitive creatures. They immediately go for the light, eh? Clearcutting totally destroys the canopy. You manipulate your canopy so to make those trees grow up instead of sideways. . . . You get a better growth rate than you do any other way because you force the trees

> to put forth extra effort to get up there toward the light.
> See, our foresters really have studied economics but they
> haven't studied the forest ecosystem which is the basis
> of this whole thing.

Wilkinson's forest is alive with many kinds of birds, animals, and beneficial microorganisms. Four active families of pileated woodpeckers provide evidence of a healthy forest. His great variety of species helps to sustain tree health. A monoculture, replanted after clearcutting, is vulnerable to disease, even epidemics.

> I have discovered that pileateds actually farm the
> carpenter ants in a tree, always leaving a handful of
> healthy individuals to create a new generation. In fact,
> so much lives in symbiosis here, that the more I study it,
> the more I am in wonder at the careful, balanced and
> intricate symbiosis of all life in this forest—including
> humans! . . .
> So, the kind of forestry I do employs more people
> and extends the employment period over a much longer
> period of time on the same volume of wood and a better
> utilization of it.

Wilkinson's methods require less capital and less expense in the long run. He said,

> Regeneration is a huge cost on a clear-cut, plus it can't
> be done. I have no planting to do. Just thinning. . . . My
> fallers tell me that my cutting costs are only 70% of
> what they are in a clearcut operation. . . . Plus my fellas
> are a lot easier on the machines. They're always moving
> logs. They're not having to plow through stumps, climb
> over logs like they do in a clear-cut. . . . That's the nice
> thing. You're all working together. It's teamwork! It's not
> competition. . . .[7]

Students still come from as far away as Ontario and New Hampshire to visit Wildwood Tree Farm on Vancouver Island and learn from Merv Wilkinson. His achievement serves as another reason for cautious optimism.

4. "A change is coming"

The funniest book I have read in many years is also deadly serious: *There's Nothing in the Middle of the Road But Yellow Stripes and Dead Armadillos*. Jim Hightower, the author, explains who he is quite frankly and clearly: "I am an agitator, and an agitator is the center post in a washing machine that gets the dirt out." He is extremely critical of his own beloved United States and of the Democratic Party which he clearly prefers but earnestly attacks.

> Far from serious political or journalistic questioning (much less criticism) of their frontal assault on the poor and the middle class, the corporate powers are being widely exalted, hailed as crusaders who are bringing a God-ordained, market-based order to the world's people. They are marching onward under the golden banner of 'globalization,' a nowhere land in which honey is promised to flow to all if only the owners and managers of transnational corporations are freed from any governmental ordinance anywhere—national, state, or local—that they believe constitutes an infringement on their Holy Right to do business as they see fit. Their self-serving concept of globalization gives their own narrow interest (nothing more noble, by the way, than hauling off the highest possible profit they can grab) supremacy over all competing interests around the world, including those of labor, human rights, environment, religion, democracy, community, and nation.

Hightower goes far beyond negative criticism, however, to express positive confidence that a change is coming. "There is no need to 'create' a progressive movement," he says,

> because it already exists in the hearts and minds of America's ordinary folks. Instead the chore of progressive strategists and organizers is to connect these folks nationally and help them build an independent political mechanism that frees them from reliance on either branch of today's corporate, one-party structure.[8]

Jim Hightower is one of my seven reasons for cautious optimism because his book represents the good work being done by thousands of other writers, artists, musicians, scientists and non-governmental organizations. All these communicators are helping to expand public awareness of the crises of our day—not only the dangerous problems we face but also our exciting opportunities to resolve them.

5. Jubilee 2000 International Debt Cancellation Campaign

The Canadian Ecumenical Jubilee Initiative is part of an international effort urging debt relief as one step toward "making the new millennium a time to give new hope to literally millions of people whose very survival is threatened by chronic poverty and malnutrition." Helping to launch the [Canadian] national campaign on Parliament Hill, Senator Lois Wilson, former moderator of the United Church of Canada, spoke: "We call upon the Canadian government, along with the G-8 industrialized nations, the International Monetary Fund (IMF), the World Bank and the World Trade Organization, to listen to the cry of the people of the world to cancel these unpayable debts."

Susan George, patron of Britain's Jubilee 2000, said, "This is an achievable goal. The sums involved are paltry for us but they are enormous for the poorest people." She is the author of *The Debt Boomerang* and *A Fate Worse than Debt*. Over the past ten years, she said, the average payment of countries designated by the World Bank as highly indebted poor countries was $30 million a day. That's over $1.2 million an hour and $21,000 every minute. As well, an average of 20 percent of all the export earnings of the countries goes to pay the debts.

Christopher Mwakasege, leading spokesperson from Tanzania for Jubilee Africa, said that cancellation of the debt in the sub-Saharan region alone would save millions of lives, "lives of children no different than your children in Canada." He pointed out that UNICEF estimated that $9 billion invested in health and nutrition in the region could save the lives of 21 million people. "But African countries cannot afford this kind of investment because they must pay . . . $13 billion in debt servicing payments each year."

Mwakasege also noted that the Jubilee 2000 campaign calls not only for debt cancellation but also for effective steps to prevent the buildup of debt in the future. One of those steps should be the suspension and redesigning of structural adjustment programs "which the IMF forces on countries as conditions for debt relief and which have not, so far, solved the development problems of the countries, but instead have made these countries become economic slaves of the creditors. We are saying that this is injustice and it is not acceptable to us."

A drive has been undertaken to collect signatures for an international petition calling on the leaders of the G-8 countries to cancel the backlog of unpayable debts of 50 of the most impoverished countries by the year 2000. The petitions will be presented to leaders at the meeting of G-8 countries in Germany in 1999. [9]

For the Inter-Church Coalition on Africa, Jana Kelly wrote "Mozambique: The Social and Economic Costs of the Debt Crisis." In April 1998 the World Bank and the IMF announced that Mozambique was officially eligible for debt relief under the Highly Indebted Poor Country (HIPC) Initiative. "This HIPC Initiative is a prime example of a cosmetic policy that does not begin to address the foundation of the current debt crisis," Kelly wrote.

> Through their imposed economic reforms in Mozambique, multilateral banks and bilateral creditors have made it acceptable to open private clinics while village health posts go without medicine; to build gourmet restaurants while people go hungry; and to rehabilitate luxury hotels while many are homeless. *If we do not respond to this contradiction, we, too, make it acceptable.* [10]

The growing international concern about unbearable debt problems offers a good reason for cautious optimism.

6. Responsibility for the next seven generations

David Suzuki must be one of the world's best informed advocates of ecological and aboriginal collaboration for the survival and well-being of life on earth. I am sure that he never learned anything in school about the ecological importance of aboriginal knowledge and experience in our modern struggle for survival.

Suzuki came to appreciate aboriginal wisdom, spirit and humour—and he is still learning—through personal contact with indigenous people and communities around the world.

Suzuki is by no means alone in the world among non-aboriginal people who have been alerted to the historical savagery of some "civilized" societies and awakened to the potentially civilizing influence of many so-called "savage" societies. We may be cautiously optimistic that these truths will soon become much more available to students. Some schools and universities are beginning to embrace this important aspect of history.

Decimated by non-aboriginal diseases and devastated by many generations of non-aboriginal attempts to assimilate or exterminate them, these "vanishing" peoples have earned first place among the most experienced survivors ever known on earth.

In his Personal Foreword for *Wisdom of the Elders: Sacred Native Stories of Nature*, Suzuki wrote, "My experiences with aboriginal peoples have convinced me, both as a scientist and as an environmentalist, of the power and relevance of their knowledge and worldview in a time of imminent global ecocatastrophe."[11]

In *The Sacred Balance: Rediscovering our Place in Nature*, David Suzuki with Amanda McConnell point out the intimate connection between aboriginal experience and ecological science:

> For most aboriginal people, land has been the foundation of life and the source of inspiration, identity, history and meaning. . . .Thus, the human relationship with land requires that people protect and maintain its fecundity. Their role was not to take too much but to leave some for others or another time and to return the remnants of their hunting or gathering back to the Earth.

This aboriginal sense of responsibility for the land is echoed in a document signed by such eminent scientists as Carl Sagan, Stephen Schneider, Freeman Dyson, Peter Raven, and Stephen Jay Gould. It is remarkable for its use of the word "creation" in a spiritual sense and in its clear condemnation of the ecologically destructive path we are on: "The Earth is the birthplace of our species and, so far as we know, our only home. . . . We are close to committing—many would argue we are already committing—what in our language is sometimes called Crimes against Creation." [12]

I am cautiously optimistic that this aboriginal-ecological collaboration, unknown until only a few decades ago, will continue to gain strength until it opens a way into the twenty-first century for all human beings to consider adopting and carrying responsibility for the next seven generations.

To conspire means to breathe together. If I call this promising development an aboriginal-ecological conspiracy, I mean that indigenous and other communities around the world will try to find the best ways to breathe together for mutual survival and well-being. The alternative to this cooperative endeavour may well be as unacceptable as losing our breath entirely.

7. Waging Peace for a Living

Even the publication of this book might become a seventh reason for hope if it contributes in any way to public awareness of both danger and opportunity. Cautious optimism may become thoroughly justified when NGOs take imaginative action together for survival and well-being of life on earth. There are now, right in front of us, great opportunities for cooperation among nongovernmental organizations and other individuals working for human rights, environment, ecological economics, full and meaningful employment, cross-cultural appreciation, education, health, peace, justice, non-violent conflict resolution, community development, and spiritual strength.

Best wishes to us all!

Notes

1. David C. Korten, *When Corporations Rule the World*, West Hartford, Connecticut: Kumarian Press; San Francisco: Berrett-Koehler Publishers, 1995, pp.13-14.

2. Katherine Ainger, "Intelligent graffiti, hysterical police," Toronto: *The New Internationalist*, November 1998, p. 28.

3. The Hague Appeal for Peace, Civil Society Conference, May 11-15, 1999. Invitation to "A Campaign and a Conference to delegitimize armed conflict and create a culture of peace for the 21st century." Karina Wood, U.S. Outreach Coordinator, 43 Nisbet St., 3rd Floor, Providence, Rhode Island, U.S.A. 0296.

4. Alliance for Responsible Trade/Common Frontiers, *Alternatives for the Americas: Building a Peoples' Hemispheric Agreement*, Ottawa: Co-published by the Canadian Centre for Policy Alternatives and Common Frontiers, 1999.

5. Chief Joseph Gosnell, speech to the British Columbia Legislative Assembly, 1998 Legislative Session: 3rd Session, 36th Parliament, Victoria: *Hansard Blue*, Volume 12, Number 17, December 2, 1998.

6. Ruth Loomis with Merv Wilkinson, *Wildwood: A Forest for the Future*, Gabriola, B.C.: Reflections, 1989.

7. Susan Zwinger, "An Interview with Merv Wilkinson, a Fifty Year Practitioner of Ecoforestry," interviewed near Ladysmith on Vancouver Island, British Columbia, April 12, 1994.

8. Jim Hightower, *There's Nothing in the Middle of the Road But Yellow Stripes and Dead Armadillos*, New York: HarperCollins, 1997, HarperPerennial, 1998, pp. xiv-xv and 293-294.

9. Art Babych, "Proclaim Jubilee: Cut chains shackling heavily indebted countries!" Toronto: *Catholic New Times*, October 11, 1998.

10. Jana Kelly, "Mozambique: The Social and Economic Costs of the Debt Crisis," West Toronto: Inter-Church Coalition on Africa. "A New Beginning: A Call for Jubilee," 1999.

11. *Op. cit.*, Chapter 1, Note 31(o).

12. David Suzuki with Amanda McConnell, *The Sacred Balance: Rediscovering Our Place in Nature*, Vancouver: Greystone Books, A Division of Douglas & McIntyre, 1997, pp. 78-80. Copyright 1997 by David Suzuki; quoted by permission of the publisher.

An Opportunity for Mutual Aid Among Non-Governmental Organizations

Chapters 4 and 7 invited interested NGOs to explore the WAGING PEACE FOR A LIVING concept and out of that review to produce their own consensus for an effective "action plan for survival of life on earth."

Most non-governmental organizations are already active, within the limits of their resources, in significant aspects of waging peace. They have earned great public respect around the world for their culturally sensitive work to facilitate regional and community efforts to swim upstream against a powerful flood of unecological economics.

With a modest amount of initial financial support, a few of these concerned groups may decide to organize a Waging Peace Coalition of NGOs. Cooperating together they could empower a frustrated world society to undertake all the challenging, non-profit work required to achieve and sustain peace on earth with justice for all.

A working group from this Waging Peace Coalition of NGOs could take the necessary steps to prepare the WORK INVENTORY of urgently needed projects. The working group could also invent a FINANCIAL SUPPORT INVENTORY of innovative ways to pay those people who do all this work, even if governments continue refusing to invest sufficient tax dollars in the twenty-first century work required for survival of life on a sustaining earth.

Collaboration will enhance the work that each participating NGO is already doing, increase each one's financial and personnel resources, and move the whole world toward a more promising tomorrow with real opportunities for virtually full employment.

The following list is very far from complete, but it provides a starting place. Based on their own contacts and experience, many readers will probably suggest additional names of appropriate NGOs likely to become interested in this cooperative effort.

This alphabetical list of non-governmental organizations has been selected to include certain characteristics: international peace; human rights; ecological economics; survival interests; women; minorities, including aboriginal; and third world concerns.

Aboriginal Resource Centre (ARC)
Alliance for a Responsible and United World
American Association for the Advancement of Science
American Friends Service Committee (Quaker)
Amnesty International
Assembly of First Nations

The Beijer Institute: The International Institute of Ecological Economics

Caledon Institute of Social Responsibility
The Calmeadow Foundation
Canadian Arctic Resource Committee
Canadian Catholic Organization for Development and Peace
Canadian Centre for Policy Alternatives
Canadian Council for International Cooperation
Canadian Council on Social Development
Canadian Environmental Defence Fund
Canadian Environmental Network
Canadian Friends Service Committee (Quaker)
Canadian Organization for Development Through Education (CODE)
The Canadian Peace Alliance
Canadian Peacebuilding Coordinating Committee
Canadian Physicians for Aid and Relief
Canadian Physicians for the Prevention of Nuclear War
Canadian University Service Overseas (CUSO)
Canadian Voice of Women for Peace
Centre for Social Justice
CHO!CES

Christian Task Force on Central America
Citizens for Public Justice
Coady International Institute, St. Francis Xavier University
Coalition to Oppose the Arms Trade
CoDevelopment Canada
Conscience Canada
The Council of Canadians
The David Suzuki Foundation

Ecotrust
Ecumenical Coalition for Economic Justice
End the Arms Race (Public Education for Peace Society)
End Legislated Poverty

Farmfolk/Cityfolk Society
Fellowship of Reconciliation
Food First/Institute for Food and Development
Friends Committee on National Legislation
Friends of the Earth

Green Cross International
Greenpeace
Ground Zero Center for Nonviolent Action
Guideposts for a Sustainable Future (Planning for Seven
    Generations)

The Hague Appeal for Peace

International Council on Adult Education
International Development Research Centre
International Institute of Concern for Public Health
International Institute for Sustainable Development
Inter Pares

The John Howard Society of Canada

MATCH International Centre
Médicins sans Frontières (Doctors Without Borders)
Mennonite Central Committee

National Action Committee on the Status of Women
National Anti-Poverty Organization
The Nature Conservancy of Canada
North-South Institute
Northwest Institute for Bioregional Studies

Oxfam Canada

Pacific Campaign to Disarm the Seas
Peace Brigades International
Peacefund Canada
Physicians for Global Survival
Planned Parenthood Federation of Canada
Probe International (Energy Probe)
Program on Corporations, Law and Democracy
Project Ploughshares
Public Conversations Project, Family Institute of Cambridge

Responsible Wealth (A Project of United for a Fair Economy)

Save the Children - Canada
Seventh Generation Fund
Sierra Club of Canada
Sierra Legal Defence Fund
Social Planning and Research Council of British Columbia
Societé pour vaincre la pollution (SVP)
Society Promoting Environmental Conservation (SPEC)
Street Kids International
Sustainable Development Research Institute, University of British
    Columbia

The Temple of Understanding (A Global Interfaith Association)
Transparency International
Turning 2000, Sustainable Community Development
Turtle Island Earth Stewards (TIES)

Union of British Columbia Indian Chiefs
Union of Concerned Scientists
UNESCO, United Nations Educational, Scientific and Cultural
    Organization
UNEP, United Nations Environment Program
UNICEF, United Nations International Children's Emergency Fund
Unitarian Service Committee (USC Canada)

Valhalla Wilderness Society
Vanier Institute of the Family

War Resisters League
Women's Legal Education and Action Fund
World Federalists of Canada
Worldwatch Institute

A Draft Timetable for Waging Peace

Organization Year

Some NGOs gather to form a Waging Peace Coalition, review this book's proposed action plan, and adopt or improve it, or replace it with a better plan.

Research Year

One year of research with four objectives:
1. WORK INVENTORY—2 paid researchers and up to 75 subcontracted consultants produce the NGO inventory of essential work.
2. FINANCIAL SUPPORT INVENTORY—2 paid researchers and up to 15 subcontracted consultants produce an inventory including old funding sources and innovative methods for inviting all kinds of sources, old and new, to invest in action for survival and long-range well-being.
3. Draft a proposed management plan for a trillion dollars-per-year fund for the NGO Coalition to consider before establishing a board of trustees and then launching a cooperative campaign to assemble and constructively distribute one trillion dollars per year for the duration of the global crisis.
4. Develop a plan with a budget for five years of waging peace demonstration projects in a number of regions by using the two inventories to undertake necessary local work plus each region's share of urgently needed global work.

For details of staffing, budgeting and operating requirements, see Appendix III.

Five Years of Demonstration Projects

Waging Peace Spreads Around the World

With the benefit of reports from regional demonstration projects, the NGO Coalition will be able to spread information worldwide about possibilities for making use of the inventories or adapting them to fit a great variety of local cultures and conditions.

In addition to accomplishing work that is urgently needed both locally and globally, the use of these two inventories will make it possible to achieve virtually full employment eventually around the world.

A Draft Budget for the One-Year Research Project

> People need to be needed as much as they need food,
> water, shelter and clothes. Fortunately, in our present
> global predicament, everyone is needed!
> —Walt Taylor

Referring to Chapter 7, A Plan for One Year of Waging Peace Research, here is my concept of a feasible budget, subject to revision by a responsible organization such as the working group of the Waging Peace Coalition of NGOs.

A draft one-year research budget is outlined below:

Salaries and Benefits:

One research project coordinator	$ 65,000
Four researchers @ $60,000 each	240,000
One office administrator	60,000
Benefits @ 20% of salaries	73,000

Consultation:

75 Work Inventory consultants, at average cost of $1,500 each	112,500
15 Financial Support Inventory consultants, at average cost of $3,500 each	52,500
10 Demonstration Project consultants, at average cost of $3,000 each	30,000

Operating Costs:

Travel (staff and consultants) @ 4,000/month	48,000
Office space (300 sq. ft. @ $35 each)	10,500
Communication (fax, phone) @ $800/month	9,600
Hardware and software (4 computers and printer)	15,000
Photocopying and publication	7,500
Miscellaneous (stationery, supplies, postage) @ $400/month	4,800
Administration (10% of $95,400, operating costs)	9,540

TOTAL FOR THE RESEARCH YEAR
(In Canadian dollars) $737,940
(In US dollars approximately $ 500,000)

If any part of this proposed budget is not needed, the surplus can be creatively invested in the TRILLION DOLLARS PER YEAR WAGING PEACE FUND.

Additional budgets will be drafted by the one-year research team for the Five-Year Demonstration Projects and for subsequent years to spread around the world the inventories and the benefits of WAGING PEACE FOR A LIVING.

Purposes of the Waging Peace Society

On July 26, 1993, the Registrar of Companies for the Province of British Columbia, Canada, certified that the Waging Peace Society had this day been incorporated under the *Society Act.*

The purposes of the Waging Peace Society are:

a) To foster full employment doing all the necessary new work and stimulating ecological ways of doing old work to keep this planet habitable and life worth living for our own and future generations.

b) To prepare two necessary tools for significant progress toward full employment in appropriate work for a sustainable society in the twenty-first century:

A WORK INVENTORY. This will be as comprehensive an inventory as possible of necessary new work and ways of doing old work without exceeding the finite limits of the earth's capacity to regenerate its natural resources and to assimiliate waste.

A FINANCIAL SUPPORT INVENTORY. This will be an inventory of innovative ways to support this high priority work financially so that those who do the work can earn a living at it.

c) To plan and to implement, in several communities or regions, demonstrations of the best ways to use these two inventories to get high quality, low impact, urgently needed work underway.

d) To plan and to implement effective ways to interest other communities, regions, organizations or countries in examining the results of these demonstration projects and exploring ways to adopt similar action plans or to adapt them to fit their own peculiar circumstances.

危机 INDEX

aboriginal people, 2, 9, 29-30, 32, 38-40, 70-71, 120, 141, 159, 186, 193, 206-207; aboriginal-ecological conspiracy, 207; Hau de no sau nee (Iroquois), 26-27, 84; Hopi, 27-28; Kogi, 25-26; marginalization, 194; Navajo, 27-28; Nazko/Kluskus, 173; Nisga'a, 196-198
action plan, 3, 44, **47-52**, 58, 103, 104, 173; global, 192-196
Aerospace Industries Association of Canada, 95
affluenza, 179
Ainger, Katherine, 192-193
Alternate News Indices Project (ANI), 74-76
Anderson, Luis, 195
Arizmendi-Arrieta, Don Jose Maria, 147
arms trade, 22, 70, 94-95, 139
atomic energy, 21, 27-28
attitudes for change, 97-98

Bank: for International Settlements, 19; of Canada, 20, 133-134, 159; World, 34, 65, 90, 92, 111, 204-205
Banyacya, Thomas, *See* Hopi
Barnet, Richard J., 115
Bellan, Ruben, 103, 112-114, 118, 122-123, 125-126
Berry, James F., 83
Blue Planet Group, 7, 13, 33 n.12
board of trustees, 91-92, 106-107, (*See also* Trillion Dollars-Per-Year)
Brandum, Susan, 140-141
Browne, Paul LeDuc, 107, 156-160
Brundtland, Gro Harlem, 67
budget for one-year research, 218-219
Business Council on National Issues (BCNI), 111

C.D. Howe Institute, 111
Caja Laboral Popular (CLP), 148-151
Cameron, Duncan, 113-114
Canadian Council for International Cooperation, 57

ISBN 1-55212-234-4